THE GHANA ASSEMBLY
of the
INTERNATIONAL MISSIONARY COUNCIL

THE GHANA ASSEMBLY
of the
INTERNATIONAL MISSIONARY COUNCIL

28th December, 1957 to 8th January, 1958

*Selected Papers, with an Essay on
the Rôle of the I.M.C.*

Edited by

RONALD K. ORCHARD

Published for the
INTERNATIONAL MISSIONARY COUNCIL
by
EDINBURGH HOUSE PRESS, LONDON

Distributed in the U.S.A. for the
INTERNATIONAL MISSIONARY COUNCIL
by
FRIENDSHIP PRESS, NEW YORK
1958

First published 1958

© *1958 by International Missionary Council*

MADE AND PRINTED IN GREAT BRITAIN BY
MORRISON AND GIBB LIMITED, LONDON AND EDINBURGH

CONTENTS

5

A NOTE ON AUTHORS

THE REV. JOSUÉ DANHO is a Minister of the Methodist Church in the Ivory Coast, French West Africa.

PROFESSOR DR. WALTER FREYTAG is Professor of Missions and Ecumenical Studies, University of Hamburg, Germany.

THE REV. GWENYTH HUBBLE is Principal, Carey Hall United Missionary College, Selly Oak, Birmingham, England.

DR. JOHN A. MACKAY is President, Princeton Theological Seminary, U.S.A., Chairman of the International Missionary Council 1947–1958 (now Honorary Chairman).

DR. JAMES K. MATHEWS is Associate General Secretary of the Division of World Missions, Methodist Church of the U.S.A.

THE REV. ERIK W. NIELSEN is Research Secretary, International Missionary Council.

DR. KWAME NKRUMAH is the Prime Minister of Ghana.

REV. JOHN V. TAYLOR, a missionary of the Church Missionary Society, is seconded to the International Missionary Council for research work in the " Studies in the Life and Growth of the Younger Churches ".

U KYAW THAN is Associate Secretary of the East Asia Christian Conference.

REV. M. M. THOMAS is Associate Director of the Christian Institute for the Study of Religion and Society, Bangalore, India.

MR. S. C. GRAAF VAN RANDWIJCK is General Secretary of the Board of Foreign Missions, Netherlands Reformed Church.

7

EDITORIAL NOTE

While the papers included in this volume are all related to the Ghana Assembly of the I.M.C., none of them (with the exception of the Resolutions on the Draft Plan of Integration of the I.M.C. and W.C.C.) is a formal statement of the I.M.C. adopted by the Assembly. This fact should be borne in mind in any use made of them.

Some of these papers have already appeared in the *International Review of Missions*, and grateful acknowledgment is made to the Editor for permission to include them in this volume.

Grateful acknowledgment is also made to the authors and publishers of the following books for permission to reprint extracts : *Revolution in Missions*, edited by Blaise Levai, published by the Popular Press, Vellore ; *The Revised Standard Version of the Holy Bible*, published by Thos. Nelson & Sons Ltd. ; *Liaison*, published by the Cercles Culturels of Brazzaville ; and to H. A. Hodges.

INTRODUCTION

THE Assembly of the International Missionary Council, held at the University College, Ghana, from December 28th, 1957 to January 8th, 1958 was the first meeting under the recently adopted new constitution of the Council. In planning the meeting, it became clear that the Assembly had to perform a dual function. As the governing body of the International Missionary Council, consisting of representatives of the member organizations which constitute it, it would be responsible for reviewing its activities, giving fresh directives to its work and making necessary administrative decisions. In doing so, however, it would necessarily deal with some of the major issues confronting the Christian world mission as a whole. Opportunity would therefore be required to discuss these issues in a wider and freer context than would be possible in committees devoted to formulating policy and making administrative decisions. This dual character was recognized in the minute of the Ad Interim Committee authorizing the calling of the Assembly, which read :—

> " That provision shall be made for the full discharge of the normal business of the Assembly, but that the officers be authorized to prepare the agenda in such a way as to provide for adequate discussion of major questions of policy."

Consultation on a world-wide scale took place on the choice of topics for the Assembly's deliberations, beginning with an ' Officers Consultation ' in July, 1956. A document was sent in December, 1956 to all member organizations in the I.M.C., outlining the results of the thinking done up to that time on the subject-matter of the Assembly. In the light of the Assembly's discussions this document, entitled " The Christian Mission at this Hour," is not without significance. After outlining five factors in the contemporary situation which had to be kept in mind in preparing for the Assembly, it suggested two main trends in the business the

9

Assembly would have to handle, which were regarded as
" of most significance for the understanding of our missionary
obedience ' at this hour ' ".

The first was described as " the framework of the Christian
world mission ", meaning the organizations and co-operative
structures through which the mission is carried on. The
question was put, " Do we believe in the Christian world
mission in the sense that it is a mission in which Christians
throughout the world should participate ? " and it was
suggested that if we do, the far-reaching implications that
follow ought to be taken seriously. The second trend was
described as " the scope of the Christian world mission ",
meaning the type and range of activities which it ought to
undertake and the appropriate agencies for carrying out
each of them. The question was put, " Are we in danger of
making the conception and practice of mission so broad and
diffuse that it loses its distinctive character and ' cutting
edge ' ? Or are we, on the other hand, in danger of limiting
it in such a way that our practice fails to express the fulness
of the Gospel or to meet the real needs of men to-day ? "
The document suggested that the question put by both these
trends, which was implicit in the business of the Assembly
and was its real focal point, was " What is the distinctive
task of the Christian world mission at this hour ? "

The member organizations of the I.M.C. were asked to
consider the suggestions made in the document in the light
of the matters most deeply engaging their thought and
action. A number of comments and suggestions were
received from Councils in different parts of the world, and
were reviewed by the I.M.C.'s staff and by an ' Officers
Consultation ' in June, 1957.

As a result of this process of thought, prayer and consultation, the Assembly's programme was prepared with three
main elements in its structure. First, matters of I.M.C.
policy on which action was necessary were assigned to five
committees, dealing with : (1) The Study Programme of the
I.M.C. ; (2) The Structure of Co-operation ; (3) The

Ministry ; (4) New Forms of Mission, and (5) Missions and
Inter-Church Aid. Second, parallel to these committees,
five groups were constituted to provide opportunity for
informal discussion of more general topics. To these groups
were assigned the following subjects : (1) Christian Witness
in Society and Nation ; (2) The Christian Church facing its
Calling to Mission ; (3) The Christian Church and Non-
Christian Religions ; (4) The Place and Function of the
Missionary, and (5) What Does ' Partnership in Obedience '
Mean ?

It is obvious that these subjects overlap at many points.
It was hoped that since each member of the Assembly was
assigned to both a group and a committee, the more general
discussion in the groups would provide a wide background
for the more detailed work in the committees, and the work
in committees would keep the thinking in the groups in
touch with specific contemporary issues. It is doubtful
whether this method of handling the Assembly's dual
responsibility ' in parallel ' proved successful.

Throughout the preparatory work for the Assembly, it was
recognized that the question underlying its deliberations,
" What is the distinctive task of the Christian world mission
at this hour ? ", could not be rightly faced, much less
answered, without constant openness towards God in worship
and recourse to the Biblical witness to the nature of the
mission to which the people of God are called in Christ. The
third element in the structure of the Assembly's programme
was therefore the provision of a daily period of worship (led
by the Chaplain, Rev. Christian G. Baëta) and Bible study
(led by the Rev. Philip Potter and Dr. P. D. Devanandan).
The Bible studies were on the theme of the Biblical understanding of mission, the aim being that the Biblical testimony
should inform and control all the Assembly's thought and
discussion.

The purpose of the present volume is to make available to
a wider circle some of the thinking which thus gathered
around the Ghana Assembly. In accordance with the

decision of the Assembly, it contains a selection from the papers prepared for the Assembly, from the speeches made at it, and from the documents resulting from it, and concludes with an essay, specially written for the volume, on the rôle of the I.M.C. in the present situation. It does not, however, attempt any full record of the results of the Assembly's administrative work (for which the Minutes of the Ghana Assembly should be consulted).

The first section contains a selection from the papers prepared as background material for the discussions in the groups. Here can be found the " state of the question ", as it was seen by the individual author on the topic chosen, at the beginning of the Assembly. Next comes a selection from papers submitted by certain member Councils (and in one case by an individual closely associated with the work of the I.M.C.), which arose from their consideration of the subject-matter of the Assembly's programme, in preparation for its meeting. No attempt was made in the preparations for this meeting to secure written documents on any of the Assembly's themes from all member bodies. The selection of papers in this section has therefore been limited both in geographical scope and in subject-matter by the material which member bodies themselves chose to prepare for the meeting. It does, however, illustrate both the type of subject which engaged their attention as they prepared for the Assembly, and provides a comment on its subject-matter from within concrete situations in different parts of the world.

With the third section we move into the actual meeting of the Assembly. It contains a selection from speeches made there. Three of them bring to a focus the whole range of topics on its agenda, under the theme " The Christian Mission at this Hour ". They were delivered in plenary sessions near the beginning of the Assembly, to provide background for its discussions. That of the Chairman, Dr. John A. Mackay, deals with the theme in a world-wide context. Dr. Freytag and U Kyaw Than were asked to have in mind especially the subjects to be discussed in the groups, the former in relation to " Changes in the Patterns of Western Missions " and the latter in relation to " The Christian Mission in Asia To-day ". The fourth speech is of a different character. It was delivered, at a garden party arranged by the Christian Council of Ghana to welcome the members of the Assembly, by Dr. Kwame Nkrumah, Prime Minister of Ghana. Coming from one who spoke not as a member of the Assembly, but as the political leader of his country, it is an unusually interesting comment on and illustration of many of the themes discussed in more general terms in this volume and has considerable relevance to its central subject.

Something of the outcome of the Assembly's discussions appears in the fourth section, which comprises a selection of documents resulting from its deliberations. Although this volume is not concerned with the administrative work of the Assembly, the discussions in its committees obviously form part of the total thought gathering around its meeting on the broad questions of missionary policy to-day, and the results of their work have considerable bearing on the other aspects of the Assembly's deliberations. An attempt has therefore been made to summarize the reports of the committees, selecting those parts of them which bear most directly on the broader issues with which this volume is concerned, and omitting the more detailed points of an administrative character. (The full text of the reports can be found in the *Minutes of the Assembly of the International Missionary Council, Ghana.*)

A very important item on the Assembly's agenda was the consideration of the Draft Plan of Integration of the International Missionary Council and the World Council of Churches, prepared by the Joint Committee of the two bodies.[1] The discussion of this subject occupied a major

---

[1] The text of the plan, with other related material, can be found in the pamphlet, *Why Integration ?* by E. A. Payne and D. G. Moses, published for the Joint Committee of the W.C.C. and I.M.C. by Edinburgh House Press, London, 1957, price 2s. 6d.

share of the plenary sessions, and was also discussed in the committees. Its bearing on the discussion of the nature of the Christian mission, and on many particular topics within that broad theme, is obvious. The outcome of the Assembly's consideration of the matter is seen in its resolutions regarding integration included in this fourth section (p. 165). This is preceded by a summary of the main arguments advanced in the debate, which illustrate some of its connections with the themes of the Assembly's work in general.

The groups were deliberately not asked to produce formal reports, since their primary aim was to provide opportunity for the freest possible conversation, uninhibited by the necessity for composing agreed statements. In order that the Assembly as a whole might be informed about their thought, a ' co-ordinator ', the Rev. Gwenyth Hubble, was assigned the difficult task of keeping in touch with their discussions and preparing an informal account of them for a plenary session of the Assembly. Her report (p. 171) reflects the general trends of discussions in the groups, and should not be regarded as a statement formally approved either by the individual groups or the Assembly as a whole.

The Assembly, in fact, did not adopt any statement attempting to gather together the results of its thinking in these diverse ways. A statement was, however, prepared which attempted to reflect some of the chief emphases in its deliberations. The main purpose of the statement was to share with the member bodies of the I.M.C. and with any others who might be interested, some of the more immediately apparent convictions which had emerged from the thinking together of their representatives. The Assembly ' received ' this statement " as a constructive interpretation of important aspects of the thought of the Assembly " and commended it to member organizations. Since in that sense it reflects some of the trends in the Assembly's deliberations, it is included in this section.

The deeper implications of the Assembly's thought and action will, however, only become apparent as they affect

the continuing thought and action of those engaged in the
Christian mission throughout the world. Ghana brought to
a focus of thought, and in some spheres, of action, a considerable body of experience and reflection from all over the
world. But in so doing it also radiated influences the effect
of which will only be seen as they are reflected in further
thought and action. The concluding and considerable
section of this volume is therefore devoted to an essay by the
Rev. Erik W. Nielsen on the rôle of the I.M.C. in the present
situation. He reflects on the thinking which gathered round
the Ghana Assembly and which is represented in this volume,
and offers one person's comments on its implications for the
nature and task of the I.M.C. in the days ahead. In so doing
he helps us to look at the Ghana Assembly not as a static
event, but as part of a process in which we are all involved.

The character of the material available inevitably gives to
the volume a diversity so considerable that at first glance it
may seem to have no unity other than the fact that the papers
it contains are all related to the Ghana Assembly. Closer
scrutiny will reveal many connections between them. Thus
the reader will find Mr. M. M. Thomas, in writing on the
Christian witness in society and nation, directs his thought
to the relation of ' proclamation ' to ' service ', highly
pertinent to the subject of one of the committees. Dr. J. K.
Mathews, dealing with the topic of " partnership in obedience ", has comments on the inadequacy of the categories
of ' older ' and ' younger ' churches which are echoed at
many other points in these papers, and find a place in the
documents emerging from the Assembly. The paper by the
Rev. Josué Danho and that from the National Christian
Council of Ceylon contribute to the discussion on the
Christian Church and non-Christian religions, and in so
doing illustrate that close relationship of religion and culture
with which Mr. Thomas' paper is much concerned, and
which is by no means irrelevant to the question posed in
the Rev. J. V. Taylor's discussion of the reason for ' foreign '

missionaries. The paper from the National Council of Churches in Indonesia illustrates from one actual situation many of the themes dealt with in more general terms in other papers, e.g., the Christian witness in society and nation, the meaning of " partnership in obedience ", and the place and function of the missionary.

There are many other such inter-connections amongst the diverse contents of this volume, and part of its value may well lie in the comment it provides, from a variety of different viewpoints and of different situations throughout the world, on the one task of Christian mission. Yet it remains true that anyone who comes to it expecting to find within its covers a tidy blueprint for to-morrow's policy for world mission, or a clear and decisive answer to to-day's question of its distinctive task will be disappointed. What is here offered is material for continuing thought and signposts to those places where obedience to present insights is the inescapable condition for receiving further light on the path ahead. It offers no escape from continued prayerful thought nor from deepening obedience in to-day's discharge of the abiding task of mission. In that respect at least the volume may be held to reflect the character of the Ghana Assembly.

Yet the reader who is patient enough to reflect on the thoughts contained within these pages, and especially on some of the emphases which recur in them, often in somewhat unexpected contexts, may find them not unrewarding in the quest for to-day's answer and to-morrow's policy. It is possible that in the perspective of a few years the Ghana Assembly may be seen to have advanced our common understanding of the Christian mission at some significant points, not because it made any fresh discoveries about the nature of mission, but because two or three basic convictions stood out with freshly insistent emphasis. Reflection on these papers has suggested that these emphases emerge significantly at very different points in the thinking which has gone on around the issues focused at Ghana. To attempt to adum-

brate them without benefit of the perspective of a few years'
distance is an obviously perilous proceeding, fraught with
the risk of ' reading in ' what is not really there, rather than
' reading out ' what is really and meaningfully present. Yet
the risk may be justified if thereby consideration can be
secured for their possible significance as ' growing points '
in the Christian world mission.

The first such emphasis to suggest itself is the conviction
that the base for the Christian world mission is now world-
wide. There is nothing new about this. In varying ways it
has been spoken of for decades. Yet in these papers emphasis
upon it in varying ways and contexts is so constantly
recurrent as to suggest that Ghana was not merely speaking
about it, but endeavouring to take it seriously in thought and
action, in all its far-reaching consequences. To the question
posed in the initial preparatory document, " Do we believe
in the Christian world mission in the sense that Christians
throughout the world should participate in it ? ", Ghana's
answer was certainly " Yes ! " This was not simply a verbal
affirmation that the categories of sending and receiving
countries, older and younger Churches, are outmoded (see
p. 172) ; it was the deeper affirmation that lies in the
attempt to take seriously what it means to answer that
question with a " Yes " in action.

For a second emphasis which recurs in these papers is the
realization that really to answer that question with a " Yes "
is to be committed to obedience in accepting and carrying
through the consequences of that affirmative. Those consequences are not easy, and the acceptance of them will be
costly. Graaf van Randwijck's paper shows sharply the
radical rethinking of traditional modes of missionary operation which is required, and the travail of mind and spirit
which will be needed to distinguish between the habits of
thought and practice which ought to be discarded as we
move into this new context for the world mission, and those
essential elements which lie at the heart of Christian mission
and which must be preserved and extended in their range

T.G.A.—2

as the base of mission becomes world-wide. Here Prof.
Freytag's paper has some things to say which search our
hearts, with his warning against identifying empirical institutions with the Church and the mission of faith, and
against the risk of letting the historic obedience of yesterday
stand in the way of the obedience required to-day, as we
seek to learn what God is saying to us through our own
situation, and with His insistence that " to learn means to
take decisions " (see p. 144). The report on the discussions
in the groups affirming that " the Church, because it is
Christ's, is one Church and from Him has received one
mission to go into all the world to preach His Gospel, to
fulfil with Him His mission to the world . . ." goes on to
remind us that this " is *not* a basic principle in much of our
thinking and speaking nor in our practice." The statement
received by the Assembly, with its emphasis on the fact that
" the Christian world mission is Christ's, not ours " points
to the ground on which obedience in the implications of our
" Yes " is claimed, and to the only Source from which such
costly obedience can come.

The consequences of that affirmative answer touch the
existing activities of the world mission at countless points.
Amongst them, it has implications for co-operation in
mission. The papers that follow are not without evidence
of efforts to accept and act on at least some of those implications in the sphere of co-operation. Thus the paper from
Uruguay gives some insight into the attempt in one country
to provide a more effective instrument of co-operation in
mission, linked with and expressive of its world-wide base.
The development, as a result of the Prapat Conference, of
the East Asia Christian Conference with its links with the
I.M.C. and W.C.C. (see p. 153), shows the same attempt to
be obedient in co-operation in mission, and the same recognition of the world-wide base of mission in one great region of
the world. In one aspect, the decision on the question of the
integration of the I.M.C. and the W.C.C. may be seen as
an attempt, in terms of international organization, to take

seriously the affirmation that the base of the Christian world mission is now world-wide.

But, thirdly, these documents are insistent that that world-wide base must indeed become a base *for mission*. Much of the more detailed and administrative work at Ghana seemed disturbingly introverted, concerned with internal arrangements and relationships within the Christian community. That was no doubt in part a result of the nature of the items which had to find a place on its business agenda. But it may well be also a reflection of the current preoccupations of its member bodies and their constituencies. However that may be, it is well that these papers contain several warnings against the perils of such introversion ; see, for instance, Dr. Mackay's grave words (p. 120) concerning the danger of the Christian Church's becoming " an end in itself, without regard to its true nature and honourable mission as the servant of Jesus Christ " ; or Graaf van Randwijck's question whether our " ecumenical ethics " are inhibiting our missionary effectiveness (p. 97) ; or Prof. Freytag's remarks about " our lost directness " (p. 141). If the recognition that the base for the Christian world mission is now world-wide means that in practice what comes to be taken for mission becomes simply a going to and fro within the orbit of the Christian community, then the Christian minority will have ceased to penetrate the world's life, and will be taking refuge in a Christian ghetto. In the light of the kind of situation outlined with great frankness in the paper from East Pakistan, for Christians to live voluntarily in a ghetto is to live in disobedience.

These documents themselves provide a corrective to an exaggerated pessimism on that score. They are not lacking in indications of fresh missionary outreach beyond the bounds of the present Christian community. The paper from Indonesia provides encouraging evidence of the missionary outreach of the churches there. The formation of the East Asia Christian Conference with a definitely missionary purpose evoked many references to its far-reaching possibilities.

There are signs that the world-wide Christian community is in fact becoming a base for the world mission.

Nevertheless, one is left asking, did Ghana simply recognize this danger of introversion, or is it possible to discern in its thought any indications of the directions in which the missionary outreach from the base of the world-wide community is to be looked for? Did it give any answer to the second of the two questions posed in the preparatory document (see p. 10) concerning the ' scope ' of the mission?

It is certain that Ghana's answer to this second question was much less clear than its answer to the first. Perhaps, however, it may be very tentatively suggested that these papers indicate two directions in which answers may be sought. The references to the new encounter with non-Christian religions possibly point in one such direction. As Dr. Mackay suggested (p. 106), from its new world-wide base the Christian world mission ought to be coming into a new encounter with the living faiths of men. In this connection, U Kyaw Than's comments that " the proclamation of the Gospel has not really happened for the Buddhist " (p. 130) is worth pondering.

The group on " the Christian Witness in Society and Nation " was surely pointing to another missionary frontier to be crossed from the world-wide base. It is difficult to read with imagination the section of the report on the group discussions dealing with this topic (p. 175 f.) without sensing in it the need for a new type of missionary pioneering (from the *whole* Christian world community) especially if one reads it in the context of Mr. M. M. Thomas's simple but searching phrase, " the Christian witness to Christ as the redeemer of nation and society " (p. 23). Concrete illustrations of that frontier of world mission are not lacking in the papers from member bodies included in the fourth section.

It is possible that what are here spoken of as two frontiers are not really two but one. The intimate relation between religion and the total life of the community comes out clearly, for instance, in the paper from Ceylon. It may be that really to come into encounter with a non-Christian religion is to come into the heart of " Christian Witness in Society and Nation ", and that really to bear a Christian witness in society and nation is to be brought into encounter with the religion (ancient or modern, Asian or African or western) which lies at its heart. Perhaps only as we learn to cross those frontiers, that we think of separately, as *one* frontier, shall we learn how the world-wide Christian community can become not a ghetto, but a bridge-head, and discover afresh how to be missionary servants amongst " the Gentiles ", the nations, " ourselves your servants for Jesus' sake ".

" For Jesus' sake . . . " ; that for one reader at least sums up the fourth emphasis in these papers. They come back at many different points to the affirmation that the mission is not ours, but Christ's. They find in Him its origin, its framework and its content. This emphasis runs throughout Dr. Mackay's paper. Dr. Mathews indicates the essential framework of the world mission when he remarks (p. 39), " We have no status outside Jesus Christ, and we belong to one another only through Him." Prof. Freytag calls us to see in the facts of our present situation a setting of us free " for the more difficult but essential task, to concentrate on the message of Christ Himself and that means on the message of the Cross " (p. 145). The report of the group discussions speaks of the need to confront men and women with a Person, Jesus Christ, " Christianity's unique and unassailable element " (p. 176) ; while the statement affirms " we are all agreed that this is an hour in which Christians must go out into all the world in the name of *Christus Victor* " (p. 183).

Are these but platitudes of Christian conferences ? They were not so spoken at Ghana. Whether they become such depends on the seriousness with which we take them. In the context of these papers they are recalling us to the true centre of " the distinctive task of the Christian world mission to-day ". Whether that recall is effective or abortive depends

on our obedience to what the Holy Spirit may say to us
through the thinking gathered around the Ghana Assembly,
for our obedience in action to what we hear Him say is the
condition of receiving further insight. At that point the
usefulness of this (and any) volume reaches its end, for at
that point we move beyond the realm of thought and discussion into the realm of action. Whether the world-wide
base for a world mission which God has given us in the
world-wide community of Christ's people becomes a ghetto
or a bridge-head depends in the end not upon what is said
and written, but on what is done in response to the insights
which have been given us. Beyond the discussion there lies
worship, devotion, action. By countless acts of decision
across the world it will be decided whether the Christian
community seeks its security within itself, or, open and
defenceless, goes " forth . . . unto him without the camp,
bearing his reproach " (Heb. xiii. 13).

R. K. O.

I

SELECTED PREPARATORY PAPERS

THE CHRISTIAN WITNESS IN SOCIETY AND NATION

By

M. M. Thomas

Prepared as a background paper for the Group (I) on this subject in the Assembly

THIS HOUR

THE emergence of national selfhood and the urge for social development may be considered the characteristic features of many countries of Asia at this hour. And the Christian witness to Christ as the redeemer of nation and society in this situation assumes great importance. In this connection I would like to raise three points for consideration :

1. A THEOLOGY OF THE REVOLUTION

The Missions and Churches have no doubt in the past played a rôle in creating the political, social and religious ferment in Asian countries, partly because of their integral relation to western culture and partly due to the message of the Gospel that gave men a personal dignity in Christ and created a new community across traditional social boundaries. Even Missions and Churches least conscious of a social witness did play their part—unconsciously. But to-day when national self-awareness and the social revolution are releasing both creative and destructive forces, the Church has to ask and answer the question : Is social witness part of its essential Christian witness ? If so, what is its nature ?

In considering this, there is need to define more clearly than we have done before in the lands of the so-called Missions and the younger Churches : (a) Christ's relation to Creation which can do justice to the creative aspects of the social humanism and nationalism and give the creation of structures of social and political existence a status in relation to Christ ; (b) the relation of *Kerygma* (Proclamation) to *Diakonia* (Service) in the life and mission of the Church which again will give social action an independent stand and status in the essential mission of the Church and not merely as an instrument or appendage of evangelism. This theological clarity is most necessary as it alone can provide us the basis for common loyalty of Christians and non-Christians to human values and co-operation in working for the realization of social goals which express them.

2. THE IDEA OF SOCIETY

In *Hindu Society at the Cross-roads*, K. M. Panikkar says that the joint family and subcaste which provided the basis of Indian social organization were a denial of community, of the social whole. And the word ' community ' has been so far occupied by religious communalism for the obvious reason that religion, society and politics were inseparable. In fact, it is for the first time that in India the word ' community ' has been used by the Government in Community Development Projects to denote social relations in a total neighbourhood. This is a new idea and it has been made possible by a certain institutional and ideological separation between religion, society and state. This is related to : (a) secularization, which has weakened the traditional religious sanctions behind traditional social institutions ; (b) the concept of the individual person with fundamental rights over religious, social and political institutions ; and (c) the emergence of new loyalties (especially nationalism, economic class interests, the university and the Christian community) which cut across religious, caste, linguistic and other sectional divisions and weakened them.

But society both in idea and practice is not yet a fact ; it remains a problem. There is need for greater separation of society and state from traditional religious institutions and religious communal interests ; i.e., a political and social disestablishment of religion. But when that happens the new relationship between religion, society and state needs to be worked out if social living should have its moral and religious foundations. This double task raises hosts of problems in Asian countries.

The Church has a relevant rôle to play precisely at this point. But to-day the Churches themselves are very communal, concerned with their own exclusive interests and not with the total community around. Where a Church is the result of the conversion of a whole caste or tribal group, it reflects very much the old social structure and its attitudes. Even for the Churches a certain measure of separation of social interests from institutional religion becomes imperative if they are to witness to the idea of society in Asia to-day.

Christians must recognize the value in this connection of the new tendency in Asia to secularize and nationalize a great many social welfare interests and institutions : for example, employment, the care of the aged, of orphans, etc., health and medical service and even education. There are obvious dangers in this tendency since they come under the control of the state as the organ of society ; and the state may also deny society its freedom by bringing everything under it. But the answer to this lies not in fighting against the tendency of the state to develop the area of interests which transcend communal and sectional loyalties, but for the Church to develop new forms of *diakonia* (welfare services, education and training in citizenship) within the new idea and set-up of the democratic welfare state. This may require radical change in mission and church policies with respect to several Christian social institutions and radical rethinking, perhaps along with non-Christians. For example, what are the new rôles of religion, society and state in relation to education, medical care, social welfare, etc. ? How far and on what basis should the local community including non-Christians be given a voice in the management of Christian social and educational institutions, and in the shaping of their policies? These questions need to be thrashed out, not only in the light of religious but also the general social concern.

3. NEW ALTERNATIVES

The Church's missionary endeavour and its congregational life, along with other cultural and material factors, have awakened the nation to the need of breaking the old social institutions and of remaking them on new foundations. And the nation in many parts of Asia has undertaken the task of destruction and reconstruction. But reconstruction is not as easy as destruction. The result is large-scale uprooting of men and women from their old social, economic, moral and spiritual securities without getting rooted in anything new. It means demoralization. The Church in this situation has to help the nation to develop new social alternatives to the joint family, caste and tribe, alternatives which can give the same securities as before but on the new basis of freedom and equality. The Church, being a minority in many countries, cannot play a very large part in a material way. But its contribution to social thought need not be negligible. And it can be a creative minority, if it will inspire within its own congregational life and neighbourhood the building of new social structures, which have a continuity with the old culture on the one hand, and do justice to the new urges for personal development on the other. Especially in the witness to the nature and meaning of the family and neighbourhood, the Church's contribution can be far greater than is warranted by its numerical strength. And, above all, when people are culturally and spiritually displaced, the *koinonia* (fellowship, community) of the congregation should provide a spiritual home for more than the committed Christians, a home which can be the base of operations for rebuilding social tissues. In this connection the nature of the *koinonia* of the Church itself and the social witness of its fellowship need greater clarity and emphasis.

TRIVANDRUM,
September, 1957.

THE PLACE AND FUNCTION OF THE MISSIONARY

By

J. V. TAYLOR

Prepared as a background paper for the Group (IV) on this subject in the Assembly.

THE OPPORTUNITY OF THE ASSEMBLY

THE discussion of this subject is going to touch a number of people on a sore point. There will be representatives of Churches which, even within the bonds of Christian love, chafe at the subtle, unconscious persistence of missionary paternalism, or find the foreign worker an embarrassment in the context of nationalism. There will also be missionaries who nurse secret wounds or worries caused by the changed relationships of these times, or are strained by what seems to them a waste or abuse of their service by the autonomous Church which controls them. There will be representatives of mission boards who are torn between the demands of a changed situation and the unchanging attitudes of their ' supporters '. The group that discusses this subject at the Assembly will be continually under temptation to evade painful issues by an assiduous exploration of some safer topic. If, however, opportunity is resolutely seized, a full and frank interchange of difficulties, misgivings and aspirations may open the way to a fresh insight into the Biblical concept of the Christian Mission and the place and function of the missionary within it.

FOUR BACKGROUND TRUTHS

We have to discuss the calling of the missionary in the framework of facts which have been impressed upon the mind of the Church by events of the past twenty years.

(a) The whole world is the mission field. In the west as well as in the east the Church stands in a non-Christian world. However deep may be the difference between a pre-Christian and a post-Christian society, the Gospel stands over against all cultures, including that of the west, and all religions, including ' Christianity '.

(b) The Church is now found throughout the world. If what is said about the Mission and the missionary does not apply to all parts of this world-wide Church, it is probably not true or needs re-phrasing.

(c) The geographical concept of the missionary task is largely out of date. The Mission is not *from* the west *to* the elsewhere ; it is from the Church to the world. If the phrase ' foreign missions ' has a significance that needs to be preserved, it must include those who are sent forth from Churches in Asia and Africa.

(d) The Church is everywhere foreign to the world. As a human association, and even more, as the Body of its Incarnate Lord, it is rooted in the cultures within which it stands and partakes of them to an extent no one has yet measured. Nevertheless it remains everywhere a community *sui generis*, belonging to a Head whose authority transcends all other allegiance, and whose task sets it apart from the world. The true growth of any branch of the Church, therefore, is not to be measured by the extent to which it has become indigenous, nor the amount of autonomy which it enjoys, but by the degree to which it is a responsible Church, aware of the demands of God in its own conscience, responding to the Word of God in the terms of its own environment, and offering its own obedience in its own ways.

It is likely that in the discussion of what follows remarks will be made which betray forgetfulness of one or another of these four elementary facts, and members of the group will need to help one another to bear them in mind !

Is There Any Place For The Foreign Missionary ?

The missionary enterprise in any area seems to pass

through four phases in each of which the missionary fulfils a different function.

First, he is the pioneer evangelist, the sole human agent through whom the Word is preached and the Church called into being.

Second, he is the father and leader of the local church. This is the age of the catechists, but they are trained and supervised by the missionary.

Third, he becomes a specialist ; gradually withdrawing from the pastoral and evangelistic responsibility of the local church, he now offers some professional skill with which the young Church is not yet well endowed, as educationist, scientist, administrator, accountant, theologian, and so on.

The fourth phase, which seems to have emerged in Indonesia and may soon appear in India, is when the missionary is welcomed simply as a fellow churchman. He occupies no particular ' place ' in relation to the local church, neither in the lead nor in the background, but he is simply in the Church and at the disposal of the Church. He is not there because of any gift which he alone can offer unless it be his foreign-ness, which is valuable as a link with the wider Church and as a demonstration of unity.

Some have asserted that, as soon as the first phase is ended, the missionary should move on ; others see the exit sign at some later stage. But in fact very few missionary bodies have ever voluntarily and deliberately withdrawn ; there has always seemed good reason for staying. Yet a study of the history of some of the younger Churches suggests that the continued presence of a foreign mission does retard the growth of the local church into full responsibility. However much it may wish not to do so, the mission tends to suggest decisions which the conscience of the Church should be making for itself, and so shields the Church from that naked encounter with its environment through which alone it can go on discovering the living God. Any Church robbed of that authentic and progressive discovery can have no self-judgment and no emergent theology.

Honest acceptance of this truth compels us to ask whether the time has come for the foreign element in 'foreign missions' to come to an end, leaving simply the mission of every regional Church towards the 'world' in its own area. Foreign missions were necessary to start the ball rolling, but need they be a permanent part of the vocation of the Church ?

The Responsibility of Every Christian is Universal

The answer to that question is to be found in the belief that the Mission with which we have to do is, as Prof. Andersen has pointed out, primarily God's own going forth to the world in His Son and in the Holy Spirit. That is the only true Mission ; it is for us to choose whether we shall be caught up into it and participate in it, and so be the Church, or not. It is not the Church that carries on the missionary enterprise ; it is not in the Church's hands to partition and rationalize the task. The triune God remains till the last day the One who carries on this Mission to the uttermost part of the globe, to the uttermost area of human need, and to the uttermost extreme of self-giving (Acts i, 8 ; Hebrews vii, 25 ; John xiii, 1). The Mission is all-embracing and there is no other. Within the universal Mission there are particularized callings to here or there. Jesus Himself had an individual and limited vocation, " I am not sent save to the lost sheep of the house of Israel ", yet not for a moment did He or, later on, His apostles imagine that the horizon of His caring ended there. The Father had laid upon His well-beloved Son a universal responsibility, and it is a universal responsibility that the Son has laid upon each of us. Whatever or wherever a disciple's particular task may be, he has to see it at all times as part of that universal responsibility. No part of the Church may so narrow its concern as to exclude from its sense of liability any other part of God's world-wide mission. To every Church the missionaries that it sends ' abroad ' are the living symbols certifying that its commitment is coterminous with its Lord's commission.

To Whom is The Missionary Sent ?

If the continuance of foreign missions is based on this understanding of the Mission of the Church as being God's Mission, we must review in the light of it the actual function of missionaries to-day. Do we think of them as being sent from Church to Church, or from Church to non-Church ?

(a) Clearly in a large number of cases the sending is from Church to Church. The object of their concern is the life of the receiving Church. They go to increase its efficiency with some contribution of skill, to train its personnel, to help it to ' do something about ' Sunday schools, social services, agriculture, politics, etc.

Certainly the Church is called, both as a worshipping and a witnessing community, to embody the truth expressed in the terms ' Wholeness ' or ' the Lordship of Christ over all life '. Almost every Church needs to broaden the area of its responsibility in society. But can it be the function of the foreign missionary to do this for the Church ?

It is obviously easy to justify the continuation of foreign missions when they are thought of as supplying technical aid to the younger Churches, but such justification can only apply to the old one-way-traffic conception of the Christian Mission. (See the second and third of the background truths outlined above.) Is technical assistance the best way of fostering a creative, spiritual life in a Church ? Yet this concept is now so fully accepted that a young man on his first tour said recently that he had had to learn that the thing he must sacrifice in becoming a missionary was not wealth or safety or comfort but evangelistic opportunity. He spoke with candour and compliance. Yet can such a statement be reconciled with a Biblical conception of the Christian Mission ?

(b) If, on the other hand, we insist that the sending must be from Church to non-Church because it is a participation in God's going forth to the world, we must wrestle with certain questions.

In the first place, who sends ? Both the ' sending ' Church

and the 'receiving' Church send him to non-Church. He is seconded from one to the other in order to participate in the world-wide mission within the particular orbit of the receiving Church. How can this joint 'sending' be properly expressed in re-organization ?

Again, who are missionaries ? Clearly in any local church the term must include all who are engaged in proclaiming the Word to the world, whether they are nationals or foreigners. This unity of profession needs organizational recognition. But, further, what of the non-professional missionary, so-called ? He also must be thought of as belonging to the same category as any other Christian witness, of whatever nationality, who is not professionally the agent of the local church. In all parts of the world most Churches need some means of drawing into association and recognizing the contribution of those Christians who are engaged in free lance, frontier activities in their secular calling, so that they also are made to feel that they are fellow workers in the one enterprise, embraced by and included in the outgoing love of the one Church.

Third, why *foreign* missionaries ? If we are not to justify foreign missions in terms of inter-Church technical assistance, it is necessary to answer the bald question, Why should a Dutchman be called to help the Indonesian Church to go to non-Church ? Has he any meaningful part in that enterprise ? We may decide that his foreign-ness is part of the witness ; but most would feel that that scarcely justifies the whole undertaking of foreign missions. The answer must lie in what we have already said about the universal responsibility of every Christian ; but these are concepts that still need, if they are accepted, careful and confident expression.

September, 1957.

WHAT DOES " PARTNERSHIP IN OBEDIENCE " MEAN ?

By

JAMES K. MATHEWS

Prepared as a background paper for the Group (V) on this subject in the Assembly

THE Whitby phrase, " Partnership in Obedience ", was both an insight and a slogan. As an insight it reflected not only a ' given ' element in the very nature of the Church, but also reflected a reality already evident in relations among younger Churches and between younger and older Churches. Since 1947 these relationships have been extended. But for many the phrase remains a slogan. It is notable that Willingen produced no slogan !

Yet one need not draw a caricature of the Whitby conference. It is true that the prevailing atmosphere there was one of hope and eager joy, for it came at the end of the long silence and separation of war. It was also realistic. The existence of younger Churches was recognized then more than ever before. The magnitude of the unfinished missionary task was also seen. A world-wide programme of ' expectant evangelism ' was visualized. It was plain that the younger Churches had a leading rôle to play in this evangelistic task in their own environments. There was no denial of the comparative weakness of these churches ; they would continue to need help. It was, therefore, in recognition of the imperative of evangelism that " Partnership in Obedience " seemed to be demanded.

Moreover, it was recognized that progress in partnership did not depend merely on " human insights and adjustments ", but " in a common obedience to the living Word

34

of God ". Yet it is at this latter point that achievement has been disappointing. Would it not be fair to say that emphasis has been more upon modes of partnership than upon meaning of Christian obedience ?

Some have complained that instead of ' partners ' the term should have been ' comrades ' or ' fellow-servants ' or ' brothers '. But the problem is not linguistic. Besides, ' partner ' is a New Testament term, though used sparingly. Where it is found, it is in the context of ' brother ' and ' fellow-worker '.

The prophetic quality of the Whitby insight has been confirmed by events in the missionary environment during the past decade. These changes need not be enumerated here. Suffice it is to say that events have demanded the very changes in missionary understanding that " Partnership in Obedience " implied.

The same decade has seen dramatic adjustments in the Church itself, and these in the precise direction Whitby hoped for. Allowing for differences in local situations and stages of development in various areas, devolution is a fact in many lands. Admittedly the pace has been slow in some countries, but in the main there has been a genuine transfer of focus and responsibility from missionary organization to younger Church. Few younger churchmen can realize the satisfaction this has brought to their missionary colleagues. Transfer of property titles has also been common. No longer need the suspicion of missionary alliance with imperialism rest upon the Church.

During the past ten years also the World Council of Churches has been established. So likewise the Church of South India has come into being and other schemes of union furthered. In some portions of the older Churches there has been an intensification of missionary interest, and younger Churches themselves have given evidence of becoming ' sending ' bodies. The flow of traffic on the missionary road is in many directions. At Prapat there was planned the East Asia Christian Conference, an evidence of healthy regionalism. While church leaders in general may be said to have been preoccupied, almost obsessed, in recent years with matters of ecumenical organization, the centrality of evangelism at Prapat suggests that this conference took up where Whitby left off. Evangelism was recognized as more important even than autonomy.

It would be misleading and unrealistic to suppose that, because progress can be reported, all is well in the missionary world. While in some quarters the missionary concept has become less denominational and more ecumenical, there has been also a marked increase in the number of missionaries from groups who know nothing of " Partnership in Obedience ". Moreover, a sense of perplexity and frustration lingers in at least three different quarters—in the younger Churches, in the older Churches and in the experience of the present-day missionary himself.

With respect to the former, a part of the trouble is verbal. Almost before they became commonly used about 1928 the inadequacy of the terms, ' younger ' and ' older ' churches was sensed. Their use at all seemed almost a denial of the universality of the Church ; and their continued use, a mark of unrealized partnership. The issue may be in part resolved by younger and older Churches undertaking world-wide tasks in the name of the whole Church. But the tension is not just verbal. It has its economic aspects too. A sense of dependency seems to deny achievement of independent status by younger Churches. Furthermore, many younger churchmen feel thwarted by not being given tasks commensurate with their abilities and training or, on the other hand, are frustrated by appointments to responsibilities for which they have had inadequate training. There can be no doubt that some of the excesses of nationalism ' spill over ' into the life of the Church in any country. Churches, just as nations, want to be independent, but independence in the sense of isolation is impossible in the light of a Church throughout the world. It may be readily forgotten that the virtue of a Church does not lie in its being Asian or African but in its being Christian *and* Asian or African ; or Christian *and* European or American, for that matter.

Perplexity is present also among the older Churches. They cannot dissociate themselves from their heritage both of missionary achievements and shortcomings in the past. One of their problems nowadays is how to be helpful to younger Churches without hindering. The magnitude of ' unfinished business ' is almost overwhelming, but how to approach it ? When younger Church leaders assume responsibility, is the missionary task of the older Church completed ? Is it true that proclaiming the Gospel in a given country is the responsibility only of Christians living there without the help of others ? If so, then the very presuppositions upon which modern missions were instituted appear to be called into question.

Turning to the western missionary, in many areas his frustration is more acute than ever. In some places he feels under the threat of being eliminated by governments for nationalistic reasons or even by the Church itself, distorted by nationalistic considerations. He must carry the unhappy connotation associated with the name ' missionary ' in some circles both inside and outside the Church. His ' foreign-ness ' which could make the valuable contribution of objec-tivity has become a serious hindrance. He comes eager to serve and is often given little scope for service. Though his skill may be needed, he is often made to feel he is not wanted. If greater discipline is required on his part, then that is the very quality his western temperament and training has failed to provide. At one extreme he may be advised to " have nothing to do—either directly or indirectly—with purely evangelistic activities, i.e., the preaching of the Gospel to non-Christians with a view to enlisting them in the Christian Church ". At the other extreme, he is described as " a man or woman who withdraws without separating ; who leads without occupying the first place ; who gives without making the receiver feel he is receiving ; who con-tinuously slaves but without ever getting tired ; who is busy in the King's business but with unhurried pace . . . ; who has denominational relation but ecumenical loyalty ". His is a vocational dilemma.

Inadequate as this analysis may be, at least it shows that " Partnership in Obedience " has not yet been sufficiently realized. Before we can go further we must go deeper. How is this to be done ? Without abandoning pragmatic approaches surely fuller progress in partnership depends upon fuller realization of the spiritual reality of that partnership. And, in turn, that realization depends on a fuller understanding of Christian obedience—not just to the Great Commission—but to the Word of God heard with compliance and submission, as the word ' obedience ' suggests literally.

For instruction on this problem one may turn to Paul's Second Corinthian letter, especially chapters 1 to 9. This is not to imply that there is not help elsewhere in the New Testament. While admitting the perils of equating a first-century situation with our own, nevertheless it may be doubted that in any other part of the New Testament there is to be found more direct light on the missionary relationship. The instructiveness of this letter is for the whole Church ; that is, there is no need to equate Paul with the missionary and the Corinthians with younger churchmen. The relationship is the focal issue. Whitby spoke of partnership in personnel, in finance, in policy, in administration ; Paul will be found in this letter not to have neglected any one of these phases. Moreover, he writes of *sharing* both sufferings and comfort (i, 7) ; pleads for mutual understanding and mutual pride (i, 13–14) ; speaks of " not lording it over you " but " working with you " (i, 24). That there was tension between Paul and the church at Corinth is evident. They accused him of pride (iii, 1) and of lack of sincerity (i, 17 ff.). The Apostle, on his part, had been most severe in his judgment of the church (ii, 3–4).

What, now, is *our* situation ? Would it be too much to say that we have outlived a period in which the older Church was expected to say ' No ' and the younger Church ' Yes ' ;

and are in a period in which the older Church says ' Yes '
and the younger Church ' No ' ? (i, 17 *Greek*, " Yes !
Yes ! ", " No ! No ! "). But have we reached that stage
of maturity where ' Yes ' *and* ' No ' may be used freely by
both parties, so that true Christian conversation and true
Christian community may be realized because all have heard
the ' Yes ' of God through Jesus Christ ? We have no status
outside Jesus Christ and we belong to one another only
through Him. We need one another because only our
brother can speak the Word of acceptance to us, blinded as
we are by our own situation. Can the younger Church
accept the older Church with all its pride, its shortcomings,
its heritage, its guilt by association ? Can the older Church
accept the younger Church in spite of its smallness, its weakness, its spirit of independence ? By ' accept ', conformity
is not implied, but mutual respect for selfhood. Is it not a
fact that we do not fully accept ourselves nor our brothers
and so partnership in the Gospel is inadequately realized ?
Surely this is possible only as each accepts the other because
all are accepted by Him. This is partnership in obedience !

This misunderstanding between missionary and church at
Corinth became the occasion of a deeper understanding of
the nature of the Christian ministry, which was theirs in
common. Paul expounds this in 2 Corinthians ii. 14–vi, 10.
This heritage too belongs to all of us. Immediately we are
all disarmed, " For what we preach is not ourselves, but
Jesus Christ as Lord " (iv, 5). Our very ministry unites us.
For it " is from God, who through Christ reconciled us to
himself and gave us the ministry of reconciliation " (v, 18).
To accept this grace together is partnership in obedience !

Finally, Christian community and Christian ministry are
not divorced from Christian giving (2 Cor. viii. 9). Here
self-support is not the issue. Nor is there room for the plea
of poverty nor for pride in earthly wealth. For all have
received of the grace of our Lord Jesus Christ, who though
he was rich yet for our sakes he became poor, so that by his
poverty we might become rich (viii, 9). True Christian

giving is the " willing gift " (ix, 5) of the " cheerful giver " (ix, 7) who first gives himself to the Lord (viii. 5) in response to God's " inexpressible gift " (ix. 15) to all men. The whole missionary undertaking would profit greatly by profound reflection upon what is the meaning of the giving and receiving to a gift. To bring our whole service into conformity with that meaning is partnership in obedience !

A more far-reaching obedience in such terms as suggested above is called for. Christians must be one in their obedience with that mutality, which characterized the relationship of Jesus and the Father, if the world is to believe that our Lord has been sent (John xvii). Such obedience will lead towards the solution of the problems and tensions outlined herein. But can the missionary programme of the Church save its ' life ' without losing its life as it has known it ? And can the Church do that except as it remembers the One who gave His life for us all ? Perhaps only as together we obey " Do this ! " can we completely obey " Go Ye ! "

Scripture quotations are from the Revised Standard Version. They are taken from 2 Corinthians unless otherwise indicated.

September, 1957.

ENCOUNTER BETWEEN CHRISTIAN AND NON-CHRISTIAN

By

JOSUÉ DANHO

(Translated from the French original)

Prepared as a background paper for the Group (III) on " The Christian Church and non-Christian Religions." The author was requested to write from his own experience of the " encounter " and not on the subject in general. The Group also had as background material Prof. Freytag's pamphlet, " The Gospel and the Religions ".[1]

AFRICA is in the process of gaining its freedom, and trying to establish its identity and affirm its nationhood (let there be no misunderstanding—I welcome this emancipation), and it seems fairly clear that in such a situation, sooner or later there will be a revival of the old religions. For example, the growth of the so-called " Harris " sect in the Ivory Coast between 1946 and 1951 sprang in large measure from the political situation at that time, when there was a longing for truly African organizations. Does not the resurgence of Buddhism at the present time in the east, with its missionary aims, justify our fears ? There are always tares among the wheat. The Christian Church in Africa should study these problems straight away and decide on its course of action before it is too late.

There is in traditional African religion a conception of the incarnation of the gods. The gods always manifest themselves in human form, but in two different ways : namely, apparition and incarnation. In the first case the gods assume human form without any human intervention. The spirit of a stream or a rock becomes visible as a man and goes wandering through the forests and villages. In the second

---

[1] I.M.C. Research Pamphlet, No. 5. S.C.M. Press. 1957.

example, spiritual beings and spirits of the dead return to life by being born again physically. For example, albinos are supposed to be the incarnation of the gods of the white ants. In Equatorial Africa local beliefs attribute the origin of twins to the incarnation of the river gods. Mr. Lheyet Gboka writes : " According to tradition, twins belong to the race of beings which inhabit the rivers, known as the ' Ilima ', which have the body of a man and the tail of a fish. Apparitions which appear on earth in human form are the offspring of these creatures. But men mistrust the ' Ilima ', who in turn do everything they can to avoid humans. Nevertheless they have a strong desire to participate in human society and so they frequently come back, but in the form of babies. They enter the womb of certain women in order to be born, but they can always be recognized, as they are always twins. . . . These infants are holy. They are regarded as spirits in human form." [1]

Our forefathers have also handed down from generation to generation a belief in the return of the dead to physical life (for which we might use the term ' resurrection '), in order to explain the problem of life beyond the grave and the immortality of the soul. The dead, they say, continue to live under the earth, and remain in an unbroken relationship with the living, who send them clothes and money through those who in death go to join them in the home of the dead. Anyone who dies is certain of meeting again relations who have preceded him. Some of them come back to life, taking on a body more or less similar to their first, which has turned to dust. Their physical characteristics remain the same, but they deliberately veil their outward appearance by taking the shape of another person. The local idiom is : " He is clothed in the skin of another." In legends, people are said to return to life far from the place where they were buried.

These beliefs are still deep-rooted and have many sup-

[1] From an article in *Liaison*, bi-monthly periodical of the " Cercles Culturels " of French Equatorial Africa, Brazzaville.

porters. A friend, who now lives about 100 kms. from the village where he was born, told me how he recently entertained one of these beings. " Last February," he said, " a stranger whom I had never met before came to the house. He introduced himself as an old friend. I could not remember having seen him before, but he insisted that we had met, without describing the occasion. My wife followed our conversation closely without joining in ; she seemed to be under a kind of spell. When the stranger had left, she remarked to me on the resemblance between the stranger and a fellow-countryman who had died years before ; they had the same voice and the same lameness in the left leg. I remembered this and recognized him." It seems as if a mysterious invisible power dominated the scene and prevented the couple from asking questions. The impression created by the incident was so strong that the couple believed a dead person had really returned to the life of the body. These beliefs will one day break out like an explosion to stand in the way of Christian teaching.

Very often, conversations between Christians and non-Christians turn to the field of social questions, where non-Christians regard Christianity as a force disruptive of native customs. Among other things, the non-Christian points to the Christian attitude with regard to social practices such as African medicine and initiation rites.

African medicine is practised by a class of specialists whom the Africans call ' doctors ' (' médecins '). Westerners call them ' witch-doctors ' (' devin-guérisseurs ')—an apt title, since they do play the double rôle. The witch-doctors have a wide knowledge of very effective herbal medicines, and there are some who can knit a fracture in fifteen days. The cure is effected much faster than in the surgical unit of a hospital. But the treatment is accompanied by magic. The ' doctor ' claims to be able to get in touch with the occult powers by means of divination, and promises that he can find out from the spirits the cause of his client's sufferings and the treatment to be prescribed. This practice of divination and the provision of amulets to protect the patient against the evil powers of sorcerers, which accompany the practice of what may properly be called medicine, are incompatible with Christian belief. The Christian Church has fought against this use of magic, and this attack upon witch-doctors has led in many places to the decline of African medicine. Witch-doctors converted to Christianity abandon their profession and refuse to prescribe the herbs which are known to them, because they are connected with magic. One might say the same in connection with the initiation ceremonies by which young people pass from adolescence to manhood. They also have been looked upon as pagan customs incompatible with the Gospel. Having considered these things, the pagan comes to the conclusion that Christianity is an alien religion which breaks down traditional customs. He has declared war against it, and will fight against evangelization with new weapons and new methods.

In the face of these problems there are two positions which we must adopt : we must maintain our attitude unshaken, but reconsider our tactics.

Christianity is a revolutionary religion and a transforming one. It cannot give way to anything which attacks the sovereignty of God the Father of our Lord Jesus Christ. His Incarnation in Jesus Christ cannot be compared in any way with the anthropomorphic manifestations of spirits and the reappearance of the dead. Pagan gods are born (to adopt the non-Christian idea) independently of any action of God the Creator, with Whom they have no connection. In addition they can be reborn several times over to different women. Apparitions of spirits and of those who rise from the grave (again let us adopt the expression which is used) become in fact the result of unsubstantiated imaginings. The closer one goes to a spirit-man or a ghost returned to life, the further away they move and disappear like a mirage. Is this a mystery for which an explanation has yet to be found ? We know nothing about it. We only know that there is nothing wholesome about them for their believers. Christmas and Easter proclaim the intervention of God in the life of man. And this is an undeniable historical fact. These two events show the greatness of God's love for man and how He decides to save him. The further the sinner opens his arms to receive Him, the nearer He comes to him. The most important duty of the Church in Africa is to continue to proclaim the Gospel of salvation in all its purity, with no additions which have any similarity to pagan practices.

The revision of missionary policy will, therefore, be a question of method and of the means by which the Gospel ought to be presented to the people, and not a question of altering Christianity. It will not be a question of adapting the Christian religion to the customs of the people, but of adapting customs to the Christian religion, purifying them by the Gospel without destroying whatever good they may contain. Some Christian missions have done this. They have bestowed a Christian character upon initiation cere-monies, through the ceremony of baptism. All this demands the co-operation of those Africans who are best acquainted with the customs of their peoples and who can, through Christian education, help to transform everything which is incompatible with Christian belief and to give to Christianity an African form. Our new tactics will be as follows :—

1. To present the Gospel in its simplicity, in a concrete manner free of all abstract reasoning, so that the message can be within the grasp of all, particularly the peasants. Pictures illustrating Bible stories should represent Africans decently clothed.

2. To give a complete theological education to the future leaders of overseas Christian churches, so as to create a body of pastors and evangelists who can think of the Christian faith from an African point of view. This, we know, will require a considerable co-operative effort between all the Missions and Churches. Each must sacrifice its sectarianism in this domain for the sake of the common cause, which is the triumph of Christ on earth.

3. The African leaders who have had this training shall

make a study of the customs and traditional religions of their respective territories, and entrust these findings to a central body who shall co-ordinate them, so that they can be incorporated in the syllabuses of theological colleges. We think a deep knowledge of these religions and customs would help to make conversations between Christians and non-Christians clear and objective.

September, 1957.

II

SELECTED PAPERS SUBMITTED TO THE ASSEMBLY

CHRISTIAN EVANGELISM AND THE RESURGENCE
OF BUDDHISM IN CEYLON

*A paper prepared for the Assembly by the National Christian Council
of Ceylon.*

THE Asian revolution which we are witnessing to-day is
perhaps the most significant movement in recent world
history. The peoples of Asia after centuries of subjugation
have asserted themselves in a bid for self-determination.
Except for small pockets of western rule still remaining in the
Asian scene, the rest of the peoples are now free.

This resurgence of Asia has a two-fold significance. In the
first place the voice of Asia will be heard in the councils of the
world and will in some measure determine the pattern of
international relationships. Secondly, the countries of Asia,
which have been the field of western missionary enterprise
for nearly five centuries, show increasing resistance to this
kind of foreign ' cultural aggression '. The Churches of Asia
will in a large measure have to bear almost the full burden
of evangelistic enterprise in this region as their peculiar
responsibility in world evangelism.

The Buddhism revival is a very significant feature in the
life of new Asia. Apart from Christianity, Buddhism, in one
form or another, has been the only other religion which has
spread throughout Asia. Buddhism's claim to be the ' Light
of Asia ' is not without reason. The revival that is taking
shape and gaining great momentum is a direct result of the
gaining of independence by the peoples. In particular,

Buddhism in Ceylon, known as ' Hinayana ' or ' Theravada '
Buddhism, sprang to life immediately the island gained her
independence. Here for nearly 2,300 years Buddhism was
studied, taught and practised, and a Buddhist civilization
grew up long before western civilization had developed. At
the time of the impact of the western powers on Ceylon there
are signs that Buddhism was already in decline. The political
subjugation which extended over a period of 400 years meant
a much more serious set-back. For Buddhism, the period of
Portuguese, Dutch and British rule was a long period of
inactivity and frustration. With the peoples' national
honour and aspirations suppressed, and their religious zeal
quenched, the distinctive life of the nation was in eclipse.

THE BUDDHIST REVIVAL—ITS IMMEDIATE CAUSES

Whatever strategy the Christian Church may plan for the
future to meet the challenge of the Buddhist revival, it must
take full note of the causes leading up to the revival.

Quite naturally the first impulse of the people, finding
themselves free to determine their own destiny, is to look back
into the past and recover a sense of their lost glory. The
urge to resuscitate the past is the dominant mood in the
country to-day, not unlike the Jews looking for the return of
' David's Kingdom '. Whether the pattern of life preceding
the period of foreign domination can fit into the present
context of life is a big question. That new adjustments will
be required is being recognized.

(a) *Political Freedom.* Political freedom began in the year
1931 when the Donoughmore Scheme granted a modified
form of self-government, but it was in 1948 that the country
became fully free under the Soulbury Constitution. In the
pre-Colonial days, Buddhism was closely bound up with the
state. Buddhist kings gave it their full patronage, and
Buddhism became the national religion. In like fashion,
Buddhism to-day looks up to the state for support.

" If Christianity received state support why should not
Buddhism ? " is the common argument. Along with the

strong national sense that has arisen, religious zeal has come as a concomitant, since the two went together before. The state has recognized the Buddhist claim for support and is extending its patronage. The constitution lays down that the state shall not discriminate in matters of religion. However, the state has assured all religious bodies that they are equally ready to aid them, if they are willing to accept such help. Whether this is an excuse for extending support to the Buddhist cause or genuine concern for the religious welfare of the nationals remains to be seen.

(b) *A National Religion.* In a country of eight million people of whom over five and a half million belong to the Sinhalese race, and nearly 65 per cent of the total population are Buddhist, Buddhist authorities demand the recognition of Buddhism as the national religion. An all-out attempt to gain this end is being made. Christianity is the biggest obstacle in their way to achieving this end. An attempt to oust Christianity is afoot. Vast scale propaganda, press and platform attacks are launched against the Christian Church ; restriction in the freedom to construct Christian places of worship ; a demand that religious education be taught in all schools, thus necessitating Christian schools teaching Buddhism to Buddhist pupils in our schools, taxation of religious bodies—directed in the main against Christian institutions, the forbidding of the publication of literature calculated to disturb the religious feelings of people, these are some of the ways whereby Buddhism is trying to set itself up as the sole religion of the people.

(c) *Search for a Culture.* A national resurgence necessarily brings in its wake the need of culture. Although the impact with the culture of the west has been strong and some elements of it have gone into the pattern of life in the land, there is a very strong reaction against the culture of the west.

Buddhism was the very soul of the people's culture in the past, and now, in the search for culture, the people can think only in terms of a Buddhist-Sinhalese Culture. Buddhism is

T.G.A.—4

thus receiving all the consideration in planning for a national culture.

(d) *Buddha Jayanthi.* The 2,500th anniversary of the attainment of Pari-nibbana (Final Blessedness) by the Buddha on his death, which was celebrated between May, 1956 and May, 1957, gave the greatest impetus to the revival movement. This event became the all-important event in Buddhist history. It meant :—

1. A call to re-assertion.
2. Restoration of Buddhist monuments and places of worship.
3. Celebrations on a large scale, with visiting dignitaries.
4. Re-study of Buddhism on a national scale.
5. Mass production of Buddhist literature.
6. Renewal of Buddhist practices.
7. Translation of the Pali Scriptures into Sinhalese, making the scriptures available to all alike.
8. A start on the compilation of a Buddhist encyclopedia.
9. Exhibitions of Buddhist art, and the exposition of Buddhist relics.
10. Setting up of new councils for the administration and organization of Buddhist affairs.
11. The holding of the Sixth Great World Council for the recension of the Tripitaka, and conferring together on future plans.
12. Recruitment into the priesthood.
13. A growing sense of unity between Buddhist countries throughout Asia.
14. A movement towards the unification of the Sects.
15. Buddhist missionary movements.

(e) *The Christian Challenge.* Among other causes for the revival of Buddhism, we cannot fail to mention the challenge of the Christian Gospel. Buddhist resurgence to-day is very much in the nature of a counter-challenge to the Christian Church. The depth of Buddhist thought and feeling on this can be well gauged in the Report of the Buddhist Committee of Inquiry, published in 1956 under the title *The Betrayal of*

Buddhism. Although the Roman Church in particular is heavily attacked, the Christian Church as a whole receives very severe criticism. There is significantly an absence of any kind of reference to other religions in this report.

The Christian Church is suspect and looked upon with disfavour because it is understood in relation to foreign domination. The Church is considered a relic of imperial rule.

The cry of ' proselytization ' has been raised, challenging the right of the Church to engage in this and so to disturb the faith of the vast majority of the community. (The Christians make nearly 9 per cent of the total number of inhabitants, of which the Protestants number approximately 1·4 per cent.)

THE FUTURE OF CHRISTIAN EVANGELISM

The revival that is taking place within Buddhism in Ceylon is not in the shape of a return to orthodoxy, but of a very distinct movement away from some of its more orthodox views. The foundation belief of the vanity or the ' nothing-ness ' of life, which branded Buddhism as a philosophy of ' pessimism ', is very little stressed to-day. The changed conditions of life to-day, the social revolution that is taking place, the impact of the Christian Gospel are perhaps the main causes that are influencing a revolution in Buddhist thought of the present day.

Buddhist Eclecticism. Trends in Buddhism to-day reveal a strong tendency towards eclecticism. Buddhism has not been able to rid itself of Hindu influence, although Buddhism arose as a protest against Hinduism. Belief in the supernatural, which has no place in orthodox Buddhism, is to-day becom-ing a feature within it. The worship of deities is a growing practice among Buddhists—lay and ordained. Buddha himself is on the verge of being deified and worshipped. Christian organizations are being copied and Christian values are being incorporated in the interpretation of Buddhist morality and its practice. Buddhism is distinctly changing from a world-renouncing, life-negating system into a world-affirming and life-elevating way of life.

This eclectic trend can be a danger to the preaching of the Christian Gospel by robbing it of its distinctiveness, but at the same time this tendency can be a new opportunity of far-reaching value in getting the Christian Gospel across to the Buddhist.

This change to which Buddhism is fast yielding is at once an admission that the basic philosophy of the Buddha can find no place in the thought-life of the world to-day, and Buddhism is in danger of losing its claim to be a philosophy of life, and descending into a ' moralism '.

Moralism versus Religion. The Buddhist revival of to-day is in effect an effort to meet the moral needs of mankind by presenting Buddhism as an excellent moral system. As a system of morality, Buddhism is perhaps one of the noblest, and Buddha's moral insight does command respect. A world shattered by two world wars, with moral chaos, fear, hatred, suspicion and restlessness, is excellent ground for presenting Buddhism as the ' hope of mankind '. That Buddhism has gained some results in different countries cannot be denied.

However, the crucial question whether a ' moral code ' alone can be the ultimate hope of mankind must be faced. That moral precepts alone can finally and fully satisfy mankind and heal its ills remains to be seen. Buddhism has rightly guessed that the world is on the verge of moral collapse, but is its offer the one hope of averting this collapse ? Moral collapse is only a symptom of a more serious involvement of mankind in this world, and the appeal to ethical goodness can act more as a temporary palliative.

Buddhism is strictly an atheistic system, and its atheism has resulted in dragging it down to most degrading levels of superstition. Denied a life-elevating means of expressing men's supernatural leanings, the soul-destroying animism of pre-Buddhist Ceylon has through 2,000 years continued to supply the supernatural element for the ordinary worshipper. For two thousand years Buddhism has failed to arrest this tendency among its adherents.   Nor has serious crime in the country been suppressed in spite of the moral demands of Buddhism.   It must be admitted that Ceylon has one of the highest crime-rates in the world.   Of course, Buddhists blame Christianity and the west for this.

Buddhism is torn between two factors—a moral need on one side and a spiritual need on the other, and there can be no happy combination of the two unless Buddha becomes God !

The Christian Gospel is unique in this, that morality and religion are not separate but become one whole in the individual and corporate life.   After a period of skirmishing between the faiths it will certainly follow that the Christian Gospel will claim recognition by the Buddhists.

The Christian Approach

1. *Apologetics and Christian Literature.*   Future conversions into Christianity will come not by way of constraint or material inducement but through conviction.   Apologetics will have to play an important part in this.   Christian thought and language still remain somewhat of a barrier in getting the message across to the Buddhist mind.   Christian terms need to be set in thought-form and language that will be easily understood by the Buddhist.   How satisfactory it is to present Christian truth in Buddhist terminology needs to be investigated.   Christian literature specially designed and written with the Buddhist need in view should play an important part in communicating the Christian Gospel.

2. *Indigenization.*   The Christian Church cannot ignore the spirit of nationalism, and the country's aspiration for a culture more suited to national characteristics.   Deep sympathy with and a right understanding of these urges in the nation's life is a ' must ' in the Church's future planning.   Christianity cannot hope to dissociate itself from the life of the nation and yet win the nation's heart.   The ' foreignness ' of the Church's life is even looked upon with a certain amount of repulsion.

To do this without surrendering what is essentially Christian and distinctive in its life, and without compromising with irreconcilable factors in Buddhism, will require very special study.

3. *Social Witness.* Christianity in this land has been characterized by its social welfare work. The Church can rightly claim to have given the lead in this. Social service has been one of the effective ways of communicating the Christian Gospel. This is no longer the prerogative of the Christian Church. Buddhists are fast building up their social service agencies as a direct move against Christian institutions. Social action is inseparable from evangelism, and the Church can still maintain a lead in this field by the very spirit of its social witness.

4. *Schools.* Educational institutions once held a significant place in the total evangelistic task of the Church. Very sweeping and major educational changes are taking place with a move towards state control. No longer can Christianity be taught to non-Christians in our schools. The Church has been driven to re-think the whole educational set-up.

5. *Church and State.* In the parliamentary system of Government which Ceylon is following, it is to be expected that the Goverment will be predominantly Buddhist. The Church has refused representation on a communal basis. The Buddhist clergy, numbering over 15,000, has become a very powerful factor in politics, and the Government cannot ignore their influence in the electorates and at the centre of the Government. Privileges, facilities and opportunities which the Church once enjoyed are being denied. Whether state control will eventually come in is a possibility not to be ruled out. A proposal by the Government for setting up an Inter-Religions Committee to advise the Government with regard to help required from Government, is under consideration by the National Christian Council.

6. *Church Union.* The union of the Churches was mooted twenty-three years ago, and a decision one way or the other

will come within the next ten years. The scheme in its final form is receiving the attention of the Churches concerned. In the present context, the decision will greatly determine the Church's future task in Ceylon. If the Churches give prior consideration to denominational prestige and security without realistically facing the new challenge to the whole Church, our evangelistic task will go by default. That denominational differences have been an obstacle to evangelism cannot be denied. A united Church with fresh resources, greater richness of life and worship, more authoritative and powerful, bearing a united witness cannot fail to be God's effective instrument in this critical hour.

September, 1957.

THE DISTINCTIVE TASK OF THE CHRISTIAN WORLD MISSION IN INDONESIA

A paper for the Assembly, prepared under the authority of the National Council of Churches in Indonesia

1. THE MEANING OF THE CHRISTIAN MISSION TO-DAY

WE must conceive of missions in a total or comprehensive sense in order properly to fulfil our responsibilities as Christians and as a Christian community.

(1) *We must proclaim the Gospel to those outside the borders of the Church.*

The Protestant community in Indonesia totals 3,286,265 baptized members in a total estimated population of 84 millions. The remainder of our people are Muslims (66,286,596), Roman Catholics (1,080,438), Buddhists (1,500,000), Hindus on Bali (1,386,349), other Buddhist sects (3,500,000), and Mystics (439,680).[1] The balance of the population is animistic, following the simple folk religion of their respective areas. We, the Churches of Indonesia, have accepted the responsibility for proclaiming the Gospel to all these outside the Christian family. This cannot be fulfilled properly unless we are undergirded by the world Protestant community.

[1] We offer these statistics only as an illustration of the relative strength of the different religious groups, and of the animistic potential within the nation. We believe they give undue importance to the size of the Muslim community. The Communist party polled over 20 per cent of the votes in the first national elections in 1955. In the 1957 elections on Java, which presumably is overwhelmingly Islamic, the Communist party emerged first or second in most of the areas. Each voter who punched the Communist symbol on the ballot ignored the two major Muslim parties, the Masjumi and the Nahdatul Ulama, as well as several smaller Islamic parties. In view of the strong anti-Communist propaganda of the Muslim parties, this selection by the voters of the Communists as the leading or second place party was a direct affront to the Muslims.

(2) *We must witness to the Christian faith in all areas of human life and endeavour.*

Dr. Hendrik Kraemer in *The Christian Message in a Non-Christian World* [1] warns that the Christian Church must solve the problem of its " relation to the world and all its spheres of life " by recapturing the vision of " a fellowship of believers, rooted in God and His divine redemptive order, and therefore committed to the service and the salvation of the world ; going to the bottom in its criticism of and opposition to the evil of the world, but at the same time going to the bottom in its identification with the sufferings and needs of the world " (p. 30).

Dr. Kraemer's dictum of 1938 is relevant to the Church's responsibility towards politics, social relationships, economic life, and the national revolution sweeping Indonesia to-day. Our Churches must be spiritually strengthened to bring the insights of the Christian religion to bear upon each of these areas within which men move and work.

Our Churches are conditioned, among other ways, by the prevailing political climate in the nation, as for instance in our effort to evangelize the animist tribes, our freedom to operate Protestant educational institutions, and our right to accept inter-church assistance from abroad. One of the lines of political cleavage within Indonesian life being along lines of religion, we Protestants and the Roman Catholics have organized political parties so as to make the Christian influence felt in the governmental processes, as well as demonstrate that we Christians are willing to assume responsibilities for the welfare of the nation.

The life and work of our Church also is conditioned by the economic and social climate. Millions of our fellow Indonesians are being attracted to atheistic Communism because of its promises of land, rice and peace. Economic poverty in the villages, where the preponderance of Protestants reside, makes it impossible for our Christians to supply the funds needed by our Churches. The Church of

[1] Edinburgh House Press, London, 1938.

Mid-Java reports that even the full tithe its members render is inadequate to pay the bills, and to subsidize the necessary outreach of the Churches to the non-evangelized. The Evangelical Church of East Java reports that a contribution of 25 per cent of the member's total income would not be adequate. We also must relate the Christian ethic to labour problems, business practices, the prevailing economic morality and pronounce the judgment of God concerning them.

Our nation is drafting a national constitution. A number of Protestants, members of the Constituent Assembly currently engaged in this task, are members of the Parkindo (the Protestant party) or of other parties (e.g., Nationalist, Socialist, etc.). The paradox of their position is that while there is the need for making explicit the Christian position concerning the many issues at stake, to overstress them would be to risk isolating the Christian community from the body politic, and thus diminishing the effectiveness of the Christian witness in the political world. Since we Christians already are suspect by some Muslims as being tools of Dutch imperialism, we dare not drive a wedge between the Christian community and the masses of the people.

The political illiteracy of Christians is a handicap in making our concerted witness to the area within which important policy decisions are being made. Many of our Christians, conditioned both by pietistic and colonial influences, feel that as politics are ' dirty ' they should take no part in them. Many of our Christians are unaware of the pervasive influence of materialism, secularism, superheated nationalism, etc. They enter into uneasy alliance with groups which are committed to ultimate goals which negate the basic Christian assumptions. For instance, four Christians in Parliament have been elected on the Communist ticket.

At every point our Christian community suffers from a poverty of trained leadership. The men of profession within the Church have not an adequate informational base to lead the Christians properly, to educate them concerning such issues, nor to guide them in making their maximum witness to the whole of life. As in the nation as a whole, not enough of the rank and file have been trained as lawyers, doctors, and in the other professions, nor have the few who have the technical training a proper sense of mission to make their witness as (lay) missionaries. Though we Christians have been trained in the Catechism, in other ways we are too much like other people.

Protestants in the majority in Minahassa, West Timor, Tapanuli and Toradja-land, instead of exploiting their privileged position are dissipating it. By dispersing their votes they are permitting other parties to win elections. They are making no concerned ' Christian ' effort to effect needed improvements within the life of the areas. For instance, there is no road connecting a certain plantation with the city of Ambon. For centuries workers have transported the produce on their backs to the market. A bulldozer and a few hundred concerned workers could open a road to town, and increase the economic income many-fold. Christian laymen must be led to undertake such responsibilities.

We Christians need to make our distinctiveness felt. Yet events tend to blur the distinction. The fact that Muslim sermons tend to approximate Christian sermons is a danger. Followers of non-Christian religions adopt Christian methods, but dipping into their own traditions become increasingly confirmed in their own faith. There comes a time when we Christians must proclaim that there would be no religious freedom under Islam.

As the internal situation is developing to-day it appears that the excitement of ultra-nationalistic emotions is inevitable. Private schools (including those operated by Christian bodies) which have a majority of foreign teachers on their staffs, stand in danger of forfeiting all government subsidies. We Christians increasingly will find ourselves in conflict with Muslim, Nationalist, etc., as well as with Communists, irre-spective of whether the foundation adopted by the nation in its constitution is the Islamic law or the Pantjasila (Five Pillars). Though those outside the Christian community are willing to take advantage of Christian schools for their children because of the better quality of education these schools provide, they will not hesitate to embarrass and discourage the Christian witness and to weaken the Christian movement.

We Protestants must stress the proclamation of the Gospel to those who do not know Jesus as Saviour and Lord. Concurrent with this understanding of missions, we also must relate the Christian ideals and concepts to the whole of life within which men live, cognizant that human sin always will corrupt the best of human intentions and thus prevent the achievement of our Christian ideals and purposes.

2. Local and National Needs and How Outside Christian Agencies Can Assist in Meeting Them

1. *Leadership Training*

In our Christian community, as well as in the nation at large, trained men and women are too few to perform the jobs to be done. Because of growing nationalistic feelings, it is imperative that most of the technical services can be rendered by Indonesians. The Churches lack both the facilities needed to engage in the training process, and experts to initiate it. Foreign Christian agencies can and should undergird the Indonesian churches with regard to this point in these ways :

(a) Make capital grants for the erection of training schools.

(b) Appoint skilled technicans and experts to initiate training processes. For instance, the Djakarta Theological College is graduating men and women who return to their respective church bodies to serve as professors in regional theological schools, and as church administrators primarily rather than as full-time ministers. Two-thirds of the teaching staff is from abroad. Similarly, foreign churches should supply to the Christian university and to other Christian institutions of higher learning, skilled technical personnel and professors, who during this interim period can fill the gap while Indonesians are being trained to perform these services for and by themselves.

(c) Supply scholarships for study inside Indonesia, and abroad. Many of our men and women planning to serve the Church in a professional capacity have not the funds to see them through their period of training. Since the Government is able to provide scholarships to students of education, medicine, engineering, etc., who in return contract to enter state service for a given number of years, the Churches are handicapped by not being able to make similar provisions for students who would like to prepare for professional Church and Christian work. During this emergency the Inter-Church Aid Committee of the Dewan Geredja-Geredja di Indonesia is appealing to international ecclesiastical and ecumenical organizations to supply a maximum of scholarship aid.

2. *Lay Evangelism*

The implementation of ' functional missions ' is in large measure the responsibility of the laity rather than of professional church workers. The Christian laity must first comprehend the possibilities and obligation of witnessing through their vocation. The call to engage in this mission must be an aspect of the teaching and preaching function of the Church. Learning and the possibility to acquire learning experiences must be provided whereby the laity may be taught how to so witness.

We recommend that the local congregations and several classes (presbyteries) organize spiritual retreats and week-end discussions, whereby members who are engaged in a given type of work (e.g., Government servants, lawyers, doctors, artisans, farmers, teachers, merchants, etc.) may be brought together for given periods to share experiences, obtain spiritual refreshment, and thus be strengthened and informed to witness through their vocation. In some of these areas it may be necessary to call upon the Churches abroad to provide personnel qualified to do the teaching. For instance, few Indonesian Christians are qualified in the field of industrial labour relations ; a foreign expert on this subject might stimulate the holding of retreats for industrial workers. Among certain groups, e.g., Government leaders and statesmen, attendance at retreats and discussions should be limited exclusively to Indonesian subjects.

3. *Undergirding of evangelistic efforts of the indigenous churches*

Sending Churches in the past have concentrated upon the commissioning of ' missionaries ' to proclaim the Gospel and to establish churches. The Churches, which have developed from these efforts in under-developed countries, generally consist of minorities of relatively poor people, unable to finance the continuing evangelism of their nation or respective areas. A slow-down in the extension of the Gospel in Indonesia is inevitable unless the international Christian community undergirds our Indonesian Churches to continue and expand these operations. Some, but not all, of our indigenous church bodies are able to invite outside personnel to serve on their staffs, especially to render technical services. Most or all are in need of additional funds that we might continue at the task of missionary extension, extension both geographic and functional. For instance, whereas foreign missionaries generally are permitted to reside in the large cities, it is not expedient for them, even if it were permitted, to carry the Gospel message to the people in the hinterland. Indonesian Christian workers, and in certain areas, Christian Asians from other lands, would be able to move into the isolated and rural areas. We recommend that the ecumenical bodies and sending societies revise their strategy so as to supply to our Church bodies a portion of the necessary funds that we might pursue more effectively our missionary tasks. It is no longer possible for the white missionary to regard himself as a ' Livingstone ' in Indonesia. This pattern of operations by the westerner is now anachronistic. The resources of missions henceforth must be channelled through the various indigenous Church bodies and Christian institutions.

Missionary promotion and education in the sending lands have been centred upon missionary personnel and their individual accomplishments. It has seldom created an awareness in the overseas Church that has come into being, of the function of that Church as a dynamic witness to Christ as Lord and Saviour, or in the individual members and leaders of the Church who are the living witnesses.

Likewise, a large proportion of the missionary dollar is expended on the support of missionaries and the hospitals, schools and social institutions they have helped to found. Only a small fraction is available for the active extension of the Gospel through South East Asia's Churches and our leaders. This kind of distribution is out of date to-day in most situations. With our autonomous Churches now claiming exclusive responsibility for the total Christian operation within their areas, the Churches of the west must help devise a new formula. The formula should provide the needed resources whereby our Churches can take the total responsibility in their respective areas for ' missions in the new age '.

This new idea of the place of the overseas Church in the outreach of Christianity must become a centre of attention of western Christians. It is relatively easy to raise support for a missionary whom church members can see and hear. It is much more difficult to find help for the Churches that have developed from missionary service. Yet it must be done.

The unfinished task of bringing Christianity to Indonesia lays heavy responsibility on Churches which have considerable resources. But from the viewpoint of our own Churches, the job is even more formidable and demanding.

4. *Lay-missionary possibilities through international and national technical missions*

International and national technical missions are engaged

in undergirding the nation's economic life, leadership training, etc., at points which indirectly strengthen the work of
the Churches. This service is related even more closely to the
life and work of the Indonesian Churches, when the foreign
personnel consists of dedicated Christians. We therefore
urge the Churches abroad to encourage their members to
volunteer for service under the United Nations International
Children's Emergency Fund, World Health Organization,
the Colombo Plan, International Co-operation Assistance,
etc., in order that the personnel appointed might be
motivated and guided by Christian love and principles in
performing their lay technical services.

Without diluting the evangelistic purpose of the Church
in its world outreach, western Christians must accept responsibility for a gigantic lay missionary activity. Technical co-
operation operations have adopted the pattern of missions
in their social expression and enlarged their scope far beyond
the limits envisioned by missionary statesmen. The Governmental administrators of this programme are not properly
cognizant of the lessons available to them in the 350 years
of missionary experience. Tax-payers regard the technical
assistance programmes primarily as a bulwark against Communism rather than as an altruistic endeavour for the improvement of the living standards of peoples in under-
developed countries. They do not appreciate fully that a
full dinner pot does not guarantee automatically the creation
of spiritual resources to provide an antidote against perni-
cious materialistic and nihilistic ideologies. This negative
goal must give way to the positive imperative to aid the
whole man because he is a child of God.

Western churches should organize their resources to ex-
ploit the missionary opportunities inherent in the technical
aid programmes. Some of the lands which are partially
closed to Church missionaries are accepting technicians
under Inter-Church Aid, the Colombo Plan, and aid from
the international agencies. The wrong kind of technical
personnel constitutes a liability for Government and

Christian cause alike. Thus the Churches of the west should
challenge their members to volunteer for overseas service in
the technical aid programmes, establish training and orienta-
tion seminars for such volunteers, and establish contacts with
the personnel departments of the aid programmes to effect
their appointment.

5. *Help needed in the establishment of an Islamics Institute*

The majority religion in most of the areas of Indonesia is
Islam. Our Churches are not sufficiently cognizant of the
teachings, purposes, and methods of Muslim operations.
While studies in Islam being made in the Near East and in
the Henry Martyn School of Islamics are useful, studies of
Indonesian Islam also need to be made, to prepare our
Churches to make a more effective witness among the
followers of Mohammed.

Among the subjects which need to be studied are the
influence of Javanese mysticism upon this religion, the place
of Islam in Indonesian nationalism, and how it in turn has
been conditioned by the rise of nationalism, secularism, indigenous Islamic developments, the reasons for the variations
in the degrees of Islam's intransigence in different parts of the
Republic, and an inquiry into methods of evangelism which
have demonstrated their effectiveness. The fact that the
Church of the Moluccas, for instance, recently has awakened
to the imperative of proclaiming the Gospel to its Muslim
neighbours, whereas formerly the two religions existed side
by side without Christians feeling this necessity, indicates a
re-awakening of evangelistic passion.

6. *Assistance in the study of Christians as a minority*

Studies in the comparative status enjoyed by and attitudes
demonstrated by Christian minorities, both past and present,
are needed. For instance, what has enabled the comparatively small minority of Protestants in France to make such
an effective witness? What distinctive reactions do certain
religions (e.g., Islam, Hinduism, and Buddhism) induce in

T.G.A.—5

Christian minorities ? How is the Christian community's status conditioned by factors such as education, social and civic mindedness ? We have in mind also the gathering and evaluation of facts such as the social and moral impact of Christian doctors in Indonesia, who though recruited by mission boards, yet serve with the Government, often in isolated areas spurned by their colleagues, and for small pay. They enjoy a position close to the people, whose trust they have won, and are respected by Government and the Indonesian army. The same holds true also of Christian teachers and professors.

7. *Assistance in city inter-church evangelism*

The cities are hubs of the Kingdom of God in Indonesia, even though the majority of Protestants are rural peoples. In Djakarta, Surabaja, Makasar, Bandung, Medan and Semarang, to mention only a few of the urban centres, inter-church planning and strategy are needed to reach our up-rooted peoples who are making new lives as labourers, business officials and as intellectuals. The different area churches established among and for these peoples alone cannot reach the whole city mass.

American mass evangelistic methods are being introduced, sometimes by groups outside the Council of Churches. Pressure is being brought to bear upon the Council to sponsor them, even though the mass efforts are being led by persons and directed by organizations unknown to the ecumenical agencies. On the one hand, the Churches wish to be responsive to the leading of the Spirit with regard to these efforts. On the other, it wishes to guard against undue emphases upon emotionalism, and the limited and biased theological outlook of some of the mass-movement preachers. In this period of nationalistic reaction, the use of western personnel primarily in such campaigns is not a proper advertisement to the nation of the indigenous character of Indonesian Christianity. We therefore recommend that assistance be given us to establish (1) a department of urban inter-church evangelism, and (2) the provision of evangelists with an ecumenical perspective, especially from Asian lands, such as Bishop Chandu Ray, Dr. D. T. Niles, etc.

Conclusion

Our Indonesian Churches must recognize the probability of changes in the offing which may throw us increasingly upon our own efforts and resources. We therefore must plan our strategy accordingly, making a maximum use of resources now available, but so planning that the work can continue even though foreign relations were severed by conditions over which we have no control.

Our Churches cannot support their activities by voluntary contributions alone, therefore we must plan economic self-help projects. We are opposed to the concept of a self-supporting ministry, for the minister being worthy of his hire has a full-time job as evangelist and shepherd of souls. A number of Synods have undertaken the cultivation of copra plantations, church gardens, the raising of poultry and cattle, etc., as means of increasing support for their operation. As an improvement in the administration of the resources is essential if these projects are to succeed, our Churches must train administrators as well as theologians, teachers, etc.

Any solutions which will come out of these experiments must reach beyond our Christian community. Our Churches must also help the total community. An ill-fated experiment in rural rehabilitation in the Celebes, aimed at nothing short of raising the total standard of living for the area by providing lumber for better houses, education for rural people, improved health facilities, etc. The cattle up-breeding for Timor is not to be limited in its effects to the Christian community ; any positive effects of the experiments will be reflected in the entire island's economy. If we Christians lift up ourselves economically, we must lift the nation with us. This is the purpose of the economic self-help efforts now being made in the rural churches.

Eighty-four million people live in Indonesia. Protestants number but 3,200,000—one out of every 28 inhabitants, or 3·6 per cent of the total. Vast areas with millions of people have no place of Christian worship. Despite the great gains made among Muslims on Java, only a small percentage of the total number of Muslims (or of the Hindus on Bali) have been converted. Four intransigent Muslim areas were closed to missions during the colonial régime. Numbers of tribes (*suku-bangsa*) have still to be reached with the Christian message. Islam and Hinduism have become aggressive, both religiously and politically. They deny the exclusive claims of Christianity, but have adopted the Christian missionary methods. Militant Communism would substitute for the Christian categories of life a system based on materialism. Secularism is gaining ground.

The Church in Indonesia is living and working against such odds. We lack resources of men and money. We, the churches in Indonesia, beckon to our partners in Europe, America, Australia, New Zealand, and other Asian lands, to come to our aid, and in obedience to Christ, undertake with us the extension of the geographical and functional frontiers of the kingdom ; 3·6 per cent with God is a significant minority.

Our Indonesian churches are becoming mission minded, a fact which fills us with hope. We are sending our sons and daughters to areas of the nation which are not evangelized. We are assigning Christian workers to areas of life such as labour, government, and to minister to the intellectuals. A Chinese minister has gone from Djakarta to minister to the Chinese congregation in the city of Ambon. Batak Christians have gone as missionaries to Kalimantan. The Protestant Evangelical Church of Minahassa has accepted missionary responsibilities in Donggala. Ambonese pastors and teachers are spending their lives among the peoples of West Irian. The Church of Mid-Java is sending Christian workers to confront Javanese transmigrants to Sumatra with the Christian message. A number of Churches have assigned outstanding young theological graduates to work among students and intellectuals. At least two pastors chose to be ministers to labour. A number of church leaders have been released for political service in parliament and the Constituent Assembly. Thus a beginning has been made both in geographic and functional missions by the Indonesian churches themselves. This kind of sacrificial effort merits the support of the international Christian community on a scale hitherto not available.

While the evangelization of the nation, and the complex areas of its national life may be continued in partnership, the primary responsibility of winning the nation to Christ rests upon our regional and local churches. Djakarta, Makasar, Medan, Ambon, Manado, Surabaja are suburbs of the City of Man in Indonesia. The Gospel reminds us that they are meant to be suburbs of the City of God.

November, 1957.

THE CHURCH IN EAST PAKISTAN

A paper prepared for the Assembly by the Christian Council of East Pakistan

THE object of this paper is to explain as clearly and concisely as may be the position of the Church in East Pakistan : (1) in itself, (2) in relation to the multitudes of non-Christians around it, (3) in relation to the Muslim state ; and then to outline what seems to be its present policy and the lines of advance which are open for it in the future.

The first Christians in any numbers to be found in what is now East Pakistan were the Portuguese pirates, who had their headquarters at Sandwip, at the mouth of the Meghna, and were for long a thorn in the side of the Nawab of Dacca, till in the latter half of the seventeenth century Shaista Khan made terms with them after defeating their allies, the Maghs, and settled them near his capital of Dacca. The present Roman Catholic Church, which forms the majority of the Christians in the province, consists of the offspring of these Portuguese and of their early converts. In recent times, except among the animist tribe of Garos, they have made no significant number of converts, only some perverts from non-Roman denominations. Their total number is rather over 50,000.

The first non-Roman baptisms in East Bengal were rather over one hundred years ago, and came from a genuine spiritual movement. But missionaries were either too kind or too simple, and later converts had not the same high motives. Non-Roman Christians at present number rather less than the Romans, so that the total Christian population of the province is only slightly over 100,000, whereas the total population of the province is 42,000,000. And so less than one in 400 is Christian. Christianity is a tiny minority in a multitide of non-Christians, three-fourths of whom are Muslim. Christians are only numerous in certain very limited areas. Ten miles outside such areas the very name of Christian may be hardly known, and there is no idea whatever of what the Gospel is.

This tiny Christian minority, it must be admitted, is chiefly concerned in maintaining its own existence, and securing some kind of standing in the world. The thought is " How can we make a living ? How to secure a living for our children ? and How can we make our claims heard ? " In all this the help of missionaries is claimed, and largely found. Our schools are for Christians, our boarding hostels are for Christians, and in our hospitals Christians claim priority. Even in relief work we cannot get rid of this claim : " Relieve us first, and after that, if anything is left, relieve our non-Christian neighbours."

It is the claiming-ness of Christians which forms the chief weakness of the local Church. The desire is to get a share in such material benefits as are going ; any real desire to evangelize non-Christians, in spite of a certain amount of lip service to the idea, is really entirely absent from the mind of all but a very few. All too often the Hindu and Muslim neighbour is regarded as a potential enemy, as indeed he often is, in a land where plotting and intrigue are endemic and the non-Christian neighbours are in such a vast majority.

Politically the Church stands in a more advantageous position in Pakistan than perhaps in any other Muslim state. This is partly because old traditions die hard, and partly because a new state cannot afford yet to throw overboard any kind of voluntary helpers. But a contributing cause is also that in the minds of many people the missionary is held in high respect for his service to the community, and simply as a ' holy man '. For though he is not a Muslim, yet in his own religion he is holy, and he is not an idolator, but has a ' book ', and as he is a foreigner, he cannot be blamed for not being Muslim.

Yes, Christianity is still to cent per cent of non-Christians

a foreign religion. To Hindu, Hinduism is the only native
religion, and Islam is a foreign import ; but to the Muslim,
Islam is Pakistani, it is of the country. It never occurs to
him to think that Christianity and Islam arise from practically the same soil. And even in the Church itself Christianity
is still just a little bit foreign. " We are yours," says the
Bengali to the European missionary—" You are not ; you
and I are Christ's." Yes: that knowledge is in some. But
the fusion is not complete. There is still in most denominations a distinction of ' Mission ' and ' Church ', and even
where this distinction does not prevail, the feeling below it
remains that " We are their folk ; it is for them to look after
us, not for us to look after them." There are differences of
culture and differences of standard of living to be overcome
before we become truly fellow-workers in Christ. But much
advance has been made in the last twenty-five years.

In these conditions what is our policy for the future ?
Have we one ? Or are we just guided by day-to-day expediency ? Some people, the newer comers, have definitely
a policy of preaching the Word where it has not been
preached before ; while the policy of earlier arrivals, who
have now a considerable body of adherents, seems to be to
build up the Church and make it into a witness for Christ.
This means a fresh clearing of the site. But in this clearing
the rubble cannot be simply cast aside ; it has to remain
and be incorporated into the building ; it has to be shaped
and converted, and the process requires much patience and
much prayer.

But there is plenty of room in this part of the world for
pioneer work. There are millions completely untouched.
Experience has shown that straightforward preaching closes
more doors than it opens. " What have these people come
for ? They are trying to make us Christians ! "—and the
door is shut, and a shutter comes down on the mind. Two
things are necessary : one is to show our goodwill by good
works ; and the other is to create a discontent and a longing
by showing the possibility of greater things. Here foreigners

are at a disadvantage, because any graces they may show are attributed not to their religion but to their nationality. It is nationals of the country only, who can effectively advertise the possibilities of a Christian life lived in local conditions. So though the pioneer work may be begun by foreigners, and with our present lack of nationals must be begun by them, yet the ideal to be aimed at must always be the co-operation of both, and in that co-operation the cutting edge will always be national, though the strength and thickness down the centre of the blade may be foreign for a time. It is not enough for the missionary to advertise the Christian ideal in his own life. He must pray to find one or two or three truly converted nationals, whom he can build up to be Christ's advertisements, to show that it is the religion, not the nationality, which makes the difference. Then only will the Gospel appear as something which can be accepted in the national life, and mould it for the welfare of the nation and the salvation of its people.

August, 1957.

THE CREATION OF THE " FEDERATION OF EVANGELICAL CHURCHES OF URUGUAY "

A paper prepared for the Assembly by the Federación de
Iglesias Evangélicas del Uruguay

For the past twenty years, ecumenical tasks in these parts have been carried on within the framework of the area called the River Plate ; that is to say, it included the countries of Argentina, Uruguay, and Paraguay. Reasons, which cannot be stated at length here, proved it was almost impossible for a body with headquarters in Buenos Aires, Argentina, and without full-time paid personnel, to attend satisfactorily to the interests of the cause of Christian unity in such a vast area. Thus increasingly, in practice, the Confederation of Protestant Churches of the River Plate evolved as a body focused primarily on Argentina. This was all the more evident as a result of the problems and difficulties created in all orders of life by the decade of Peron's government.

As an effort to meet this difficulty, in 1950 there was authorized the creation of what was called the " Uruguay Committee of the Confederation of Evangelical Churches of the River Plate ". This Committee performed some necessary and interesting tasks ; but the Uruguayan brethren felt that this body was not sufficiently representative nor autonomous to attend satisfactorily to the particular interests of the work and to represent the Churches of the nation. Thus grew the desire and the certainty that an independent movement of a national character should be created, though from the outset it was decided that such a movement would maintain close touch with the other River Plate nations. This process was undoubtedly speeded up by the fact that the Methodist Church, which had only one Conference for both countries (Argentina and Uruguay), divided with the creation of a Uruguay Conference. A similar step had been taken earlier by other Churches, such as the Baptist, the Church of the Nazarene, Lutheran, etc.

Therefore within this tendency, various studies and consultations were made, until the Assembly of the Confederation, in April 1956, authorized Uruguay to constitute a separate organization, of a national character. On this basis, the Uruguayan brethren set to work and thus on August 3rd of the same year, 1956, was held the Constitutive Assembly of the Federation of Evangelical Churches of Uruguay. In the Federation, as *active members*, there are five Churches, namely : the Methodist Church, the Waldensian Church, the Lutheran Church, the Church of the Nazarene and the German Evangelical Church. In the category of *affiliate members*, that is the inter-denominational movements and bodies which work in the country, six joined, namely : the Uruguayan League of Evangelical Women, the Confederation of Evangelical Youth, the Mennonite Mission of Uruguay, the United Bible Societies, the Aurora Bookstore, the Cruzada Bookstore. The bylaws were drawn up on the basis of those of the Confederation of the River Plate, adapting the latter to the needs of a smaller and national body. We include, as a matter of interest, the definition of the purposes of the Federation as they appear in the bylaws :

Article 2. The goals which inspire the action of the Federation shall be the following :

(a) To make manifest and to stimulate the existing spiritual unity among the Protestant forces of Uruguay, and to promote a greater co-operation among them ;

(b) To study the needs of evangelism, Christian education, youth work, problems related to church and society, and all other matters related to the work of Christ in general, attempting to find relevant solutions and to offer the resources these may require ;

(c) To act in the defence of human rights whenever, in its judgment, these are threatened or violated, and particularly in favour of the rights of conscience and religion ;

(d) To represent the Churches and affiliated bodies before

public authorities and public opinion when it is thought necessary and convenient ;

(e) To act as a link with the Protestant forces of the Confederation of Evangelical Churches of the River Plate, of which it considers itself a part, and through it, or independently as befits each situation, with similar bodies in the international sphere.

We believe it is of interest to call attention to sub-paragraph (c), for we believe it is new and perhaps unique in definitions of this type, the mention of human rights. In this we have acted under the inspiration of the work performed by the Commission of the Churches on International Affairs (I.M.C.–W.C.C.).

The Federation has had a very encouraging development in its first year. Its work has included the following :

(a) Periodic sending of statements to pastors and Protestant leaders of the country ;

(b) Distribution in Uruguay of the bulletin *Christian Unity* that is published by the Confederation of Evangelical Churches of the River Plate ;

(c) Participation in the organization of the Consultation on Rapid Social Changes at Montevideo at the end of May ;

(d) Co-operation with the visit of the Ecumenical Youth Team ;

(e) Celebration of Reformation Day with a Protestant rally on October 31st (an act which will be repeated annually) ;

(f) Exhortation to the Churches to observe World Communion Sunday ;

(g) Creation, as a result of the Consultation on Rapid Social Changes, of a Committee on Church and Society, which has commenced its studies ;

(h) Creation of a Committee on Aid to Needy Churches outside the country, which will have as its main task the organization and direction of the help for Protestant Spain ;

(i) Maintenance of contact with international bodies, and intensification of River Plate ties ;

(j) Representation of the Churches before the bar of public opinion ;

(k) Celebration in May of the First Annual Assembly, at which reports were given of the work done, followed by a public meeting at which Bishop Sante U. Barbieri spoke on the work of the World Council of Churches ;

(l) Election of new authorities ;

(m) Co-operation in the study of the topics to be considered at the I.M.C. Conference at Ghana ;

(n) Collection of funds to send the River Plate delegate, who happens to be the Executive Secretary of the Uruguay Federation.

The Federation also participates in the direction of the Interdenominational Protestant Bookstore, La Aurora of Montevideo, and has taken under its responsibility and supervision the children's magazine *Arco Iris*, which is published as an interdenominational project with the support of the Committee on Christian Literature for Women and Children. As something we consider of a special character, an Ecumenical Library has been created, in which it is attempted to gather all materials having to do with Latin American ecumenical gatherings and materials in Spanish regarding the ecumenical movement as a whole, as well as some other basic works on the subject of Christian unity, such as *Ecumenical Foundations* and *The History of the Ecumenical Movement*. Also included in this library are periodic ecumenical publications, such as *The Ecumenical Review*, bulletins received from the World Council of Churches, *World Dominion, International Review of Missions*, etc. All this material is at the disposal of the pastors, and interested lay leaders. Also the Federation is concerned with the distribution of the study booklet for the World Sunday School Convention to be held in Tokyo in 1958, as well as to arouse interest and support for the said Convention among the evangelical forces of the nation.

Uruguay is a country in which all the evangelical forces are united in an excellent spirit of co-operation, there being

no rivalry among the truly evangelical groups. Therefore
the country offers an excellent field for an intensification of
ecumenical work, and we trust that, with God's help, it will
be possible in coming years to carry on rewarding labours in
favour of a greater unity of the evangelical forces, which
undoubtedly will result in a better witness and consequently
in a more effective evangelical action.

MONTEVIDEO, URUGUAY.
September, 1957.

SOME REFLECTIONS OF A MISSION BOARD SECRETARY

By

S. C. GRAAF VAN RANDWIJCK

A paper prepared for the Assembly

1. THE MISSION BOARD'S PROBLEM

1. THIS paper does not deal with the main facts in the world missionary movement of to-day : the existence and the growth of the younger Churches, their consciousness of their responsibility. It takes these encouraging facts as its starting-point. It presupposes our common thankfulness for God's abounding grace in hearing the prayers and blessing the labours of our missionary ancestors. It rejoices in the fact that no longer western missions but younger Churches are the centres of the world missionary movement. Its problem is therefore only a minor problem in the whole context of this world-wide movement. But it is a major problem in the lives of many mission board members and missionaries.

I am speaking here from my own experience in regard to Indonesia, but one cannot read many books on contemporary missionary problems without sensing the same problem in the relations between other younger and older Churches elsewhere.

The issue with which this paper is concerned is simply the question of the future place and task of the foreign missionary forces, both of men and of money, in the world missionary movement. It is not a new question. Has not the I.M.C. studied it thoroughly, especially at Whitby and Willingen ? Has not a new ethics of partnership between younger and older churches been worked out at these conferences and is it not being put into practice to-day in many lands ?

2. Let us then, in order to get to know the starting-point of

our reflections, briefly summarize the main practical rules of contemporary ecumenical ethics in regard to the partnership of younger and older Churches.

In regard to missionaries, Whitby, 1947, has advised that they shall become in every respect members of the Church they are to serve, shall give their allegiance to that Church, shall be subject to its discipline and accept the leadership of those holding responsibility in it. The younger Church shall have the right to issue to or to withhold from the missionary an invitation to return after his first furlough. With the exception of gifts, earmarked by the givers, responsibility for the use of mission subsidies shall remain with the younger Church. " There are advantages " (thus the Whitby conference expresses itself very mildly !) in property being held in the countries in which it is situated. Institutions shall be closely linked to the Church, but " such recognition of a common Christian purpose does not necessarily involve direct control of an institution by the Church."

All these rules were seen at Whitby against an essentially missionary background :

> The younger Churches are preparing themselves to face the immense task of evangelizing the great non-Christian populations around them. They wish to make it clear that they desire to have the help of missionaries from the older Churches, not only in their institutional, but also in their evangelistic and pioneer work.

And :

> " From the older Churches, the younger Churches are asking for literally thousands of men and women as missionary helpers " for pioneer work, for work in areas where doors are closing, for the training of leaders and " to help in building the Church in countries where thousands are being gathered in every year "—

pronouncements all of which may have special relevance to-day.

The Willingen findings are not essentially different, although there are some, probably significant, shifts of accent. As regards foreign missionary assistance, evidently forces outside the Church are expected to put more and more obstacles in the way of foreign missionaries and funds. Still, " the advice of younger Church delegates shows that their churches desire the continuing help of missionaries." [1] Among their many fields of service one deserves special attention to-day : ". . . vigorous entry into unevangelized areas, whether geographical or social, to be undertaken within the programme of the Churches there " (p. 77). Internationalization of missionary activity should be explored (p. 68). As to money and property : " After due consideration of each case, properties now registered in the name of foreign mission boards should be transferred to national Churches or holding bodies or to an international holding body " (p. 78).

3. I wholeheartedly accept these rules of contemporary missionary ethics of partnership. Surely, there may be missions which have still failed to live up to them or even to make an attempt to do so. There may even be whole lands where this may seem to be impossible. But all this cannot cast any doubt upon the essential missionary wisdom of these ethics of partnership themselves. The problem of the place and task of the foreign missionary forces in the present day in its most pressing form is not the problem of those missions which, for whatever reason, did not try to live up to the new missionary ethics, but of those who did do so. It is the problem of the missionary, who is " to some degree a problem both to the church and to himself ", who sees " no alternative between impeding the progress of Indian [or, more generally, ' national ' ! s.c.v.r.] leadership and initiative and suffering from a sense of frustration ", who feels " that the younger church [is] passive towards [him] " and " at times wonders whether there is a satisfying life in front of [him] or not ".[2]

[1] Willingen Minutes, p. 66.
[2] From Rev. Frank Short's article, " Asian Impressions," *The International Review of Missions*, January, 1957, p. 37 ff.

In support of my opinion I may be permitted a long but very important quotation from the Rev. Gunther Schultz's article, on " Partnership in Obedience ", in the symposium, *Revolution in Missions* [1] :

Not Called

The foreign missionary coming to India realizes immediately that he is not under all circumstances welcome. He very seldom arrives at a real partnership with his new Indian partners. . . .

There are of course many Indians—possibly even a majority—who still want missionaries in large numbers. They are mostly the inactive who are afraid of taking responsibility ; or they do not want to miss the financial advantages which the presence of a missionary means to them or their Church. But these members are not really those who represent the Church and bear the responsibility for its life. Most of those who really represent the life and activity of their Church are rather sceptical about the presence of so many missionaries.

You find these people all over the Indian sub-continent, in the south as well as in the north. You find this sceptical attitude towards all nationalities : towards the British, who have ruled them for so long, as well as towards the Americans, whose financial and organizational power is sometimes overwhelming ; and towards the Germans, who usually have not committed either of these offences. You find this attitude also in all denominations : Anglicans, Baptists and Methodists, Presbyterians and Lutherans of all shades ; even with the sects. You find them criticizing both the missionaries who have been striving for the union of the Church of South India, or who are at present working for a North India Church Union, and also the missionaries who object to Church union on theological or other grounds. You find them keeping aloof from the old time patriarchs and from those who humbly and devotedly try to restrain themselves from dominating moods and activities. You find these people among the Church leaders, the administrators and the theologians, the doctors and teachers, the writers and the editors. You find them among those who frequently

[1] Ed. by Blaise Levai ; Popular Press, Vellore, 1957 (pp. 73–76).

have been in the West and among those who refuse to accept such invitations. You find them most of all among the students.

They all suffer from there being too many foreign missionaries round about them. Maybe they are in the minority against their brothers who still want missionaries as before. But they are certainly the really living members of their Churches. And this especially makes them the partners whose co-operation a foreign missionary should first seek, and whose call he should consider to be essential before taking up any task in India. But they on whose consent a real partnership depends have neither called the foreign missionary, nor are they ready to confirm the calling which he himself might have felt. It is under those circumstances impossible to speak of ' partnership in obedience ' !

Only Sent

This statement seems to contradict the fact that most of the missionaries coming to India to-day have been invited by the authorities of the Indian Church. Indeed, the Indian Churches sometimes are working very hard to obtain visas for these missionaries from their Government. This seems also to contradict the fact that on practically every occasion where representatives of Eastern and Western Churches meet, the former express the desire for more and more missionaries.

But it should not be overlooked that in most of the governing bodies of the Indian Churches the foreign missionaries have still a decisive influence. Moreover, it should not be forgotten that our Indian partners have an understanding of politeness completely different from ours. Their tradition and education prevent them from freely saying ' No ' to somebody who has clearly revealed his wishes.

They are even more handicapped by their obligation to be thankful. Even those friends who are looking critically at the missionaries admit gladly that the Gospel has been brought to India through Western missions. It is therefore very hard for them not to welcome the successors of those missionaries to whom they feel they owe so much. They are afraid of appearing ungrateful.

It is politeness and thankfulness which make our partners

extend their invitations. It is therefore nothing for us to boast about. Our friends have not been free, and the initiative has in nearly all cases been with the Westerners. And this is, under no circumstances, that ' call ' which is so necessary to create a real partnership.

It remains therefore true, that the missionary to-day coming to India has not really been called. He has only been sent ; i.e., he is only a ' missionary '. That was of course quite sufficient at a time when God wanted to expand His revelation into parts of the world were He was still unknown. But to-day the Christian Church in India is established and this Church shares the same direct contact with God and His Word as the Western Churches. It is therefore necessary that every missionary sent to India to-day should also have been called by the Indian Church. Both the sending and the calling together constitute to-day the call and the command of God.

Even if one doubts, as I do, that missionaries are especially wanted by the inactive members of a younger Church, this quotation is an admirable expression of the experience of many a missionary, even in such countries as Indonesia, where it would be entirely wrong to say that " in most of the governing bodies of (younger) Churches the foreign missionaries still have a decisive influence ".

4. All these problems, however, are by no means the special concern of mission boards and missionaries only ; they are equally being felt by leaders of younger Churches.

Bishop R. B. Manikam [1] expresses his concern with the study of and answer to this question, " . . . what is expected of the older Churches by way of help to the younger Churches in India at this time ? There is much frustration in the Christian Churches to-day—both among the missionaries and the Indian Christians. We should not let it last any more." In his analysis of the situation in India he speaks of an " anti-missionary feeling ", an " uproar in India against the foreign missionary ", and wonders : " Is it so much that he is foreign, as he is a missionary, an evangelist

---

[1] See *Revolution in Missions*, p. 210.

come to convert others ? I suggest that the latter is the irritating factor. To-day it is the foreign evangelist in our midst who is maligned and to-morrow it is the Indian evangelist." Although Bishop Manikam, by implication, speaks of anti-missionary feeling outside the Church, his words may well deserve attention to account for some of such feelings within it as have been described by the Rev. Gunther Schultz.

I quote another pronouncement. One of the most outstanding of Asian Christian leaders is reported to have said in an ecumenical gathering : " In our days missions have to find a new dignity ", or words to that effect. This Asian brother has a keen sense of what is in the minds of many of his western colleagues. None of us has any desire for dignity in the sense of external recognition of a social status, for a modern parallel of the ' mission compound '. The dignity western missions are craving for is a full realization of partnership, a new vision of the place of their missionaries in the accomplishment of the world-wide task of evangelism ; a form of service which does justice to the essential freedom of the spiritual vocation ; a fresh possibility to " burn out for God ". Wherever this new dignity is insufficiently realized, we are likely to find frustrated missionaries and mission boards.

5. But cannot this frustration—so some are inclined to say —be easily explained by personal shortcomings either of the missionaries or of the younger Church leaders they meet in their work ? This may sometimes be true. But in the great majority of cases it is not. The problem of the new dignity of western missions is so general that it cannot be explained by some individual mistakes made by missionaries or younger Church leaders. It exists even when personal relations are excellent. It is a problem demanding a new vision of the task of the older Churches in the lands where, as we all agree, the younger Churches are and have to remain, the centres, the goals and the leaders of evangelistic activity.

6. Others are inclined to believe that much of the frustration of the missionary may be explained by his lack of identification with the country of his adoption. I cannot help believing that the word ' identification ' fails to convey what may be expected of a missionary and what is likely to further his service. No missionary can change his skin's colour or the stamp made upon him by his education. And does not a missionary's service to younger Churches partly consist in his being different from them ? " You are of no use to us ; you are just like one of us "—these are the words of a leading Asian Christian to a missionary who had gone very far in the way of identification. " To denationalize a missionary, which is what a good deal of current talk about identification virtually involves, may be to reduce his ability to serve to the very minimum." [1] Missionaries are expected to " put off (their) old nature ", including all its typically western sins and to " put on the new nature, created after the likeness of God in true righteousness and holiness " (Eph. iv, 22–24). Anything going beyond this is unbiblical romanticism.

2. Some Traditional Characteristics of Foreign Missions

Having thus attempted roughly to describe the problem as it presents itself to many mission boards and to avoid some misunderstandings, I shall now proceed to discuss in more detail some traditional characteristics of ' foreign missions ', unimpaired by the Whitby-Willingen ethics of partnership and the way these characteristics are being challenged to-day, both in theory and in practice, both by younger Church leaders and by missionaries.

1. The very essence of foreign missions implied, right from the outset, a spiritual relation, a relation of prayer, between mission leaders in the home-base, missionaries and newly-won Christians. Apart from that, these mission leaders in

[1] Dr. M. A. C. Warren in *The International Review of Missions*, October, 1953, pp. 389–390.

the older Churches had to open their church-members' eyes to the spiritual and material responsibility for the messengers of the Gospel among non-Christians. As the work of foreign missions grew, the home-base had to face many more responsibilities than those for the missionaries' personal wants only : innumerable necessities for the work had to be supplied out of mission funds and required decisions on priority and policy. Thus the initial mission boards' responsibility for missionary personnel grew into the much larger responsibility for policy. This larger responsibility of the mission boards—for prayer, and for finance, for publicity and for policy, for recruitment and for training— demanded a growing knowledge of persons and circum- stances on ' the field '. In proportion as missions drew more public attention in church and society, theologically, anthro- pologically and financially ; in proportion as, consequently, their activity exposed them to criticism, there was a growing need for scholarly thinking, scholarly training of missionaries and sound policy-making. In short, the growing task of foreign missions led them to found centres of study and direction, information, promotion and training in the home-base.

The presupposition of all this was the vision of foreign missions as a permanent task of the Church. I am not using the word ' permanent ' to characterize the duration of missionary work in a particular spot (we all know how uncertain this is !), but its nature.

Inasmuch as missions are a God-given task of the Church, they partake of its continuous, permanent character ; their responsibility and activities extend beyond individual persons and generations. Apart from superior powers of world history, only human sin can make an untimely end of their labours.

2. The new missionary ethics have, up till now, never challenged either these spiritual or these personal relations between older and younger Churches ; they have not questioned the necessity for study of certain definite parts of the world and for information of her supporters about the

younger Churches' victories and defeats. Since every allocation of missionary forces is a policy decision, it is impossible
not to recognize that a certain amount even of policy-making
has remained in the hands of the mission boards, even where
subsidies are concerned ' with no strings attached ' ! These
still living traditions of foreign missions are however being
challenged nowadays by a new radicalism, both in theory
and in practice. What must we think of this new radicalism ? The fact of its being radical is an insufficient ground
either to accept or to reject it ; we shall have to examine it
on its own merits.

3. CHALLENGES TO THESE TRADITIONS

1. *Interchurch Aid* (I.C.A.) by its very existence constitutes
a challenge to missions. Dr. Visser 't Hooft's statement [1]
that *kerygma, koinonia* and *diakonia* are necessary to express
the meaning of the encounter of Jesus Christ with the world
applies equally to missions and to I.C.A. The report of the
same consultation rightly says that " the missionary movement is concerned with more than the proclamation of the
word. I.C.A. is concerned with more than relief to the
needy ".

I do not ignore the fact that this consultation succeeded in
drawing a demarcation line between both activities of the
Churches ; I rather emphasize the fact that it was necessary
to do so. I.C.A. has grown up after the war out of the
Churches' help in emergency cases ; mobility and efficiency
are among its most salient features ; it ignores such missionary traditions as spiritual and personal relations of long-
standing, and is not characterized by study of the field in
the home base or by the permanence of its relations and
obligations. Is this perhaps the new form which the missionary movement should adopt for its future activities ?
Why not ? Or would it by so doing renounce some essential
spiritual values ?

[1] Les Rasses Consultation, 1956.

2. *Internationalization of missionary activity.* The Willingen conference (1952) made the following pronouncement in the report, " The Rôle of the Missionary Society " [1]

> The I.M.C., in consultation with its member councils, should explore the possibility of the formation of international, inter-racial and interdenominational teams. These should be composed of missionaries from both the younger and older Churches, to work on new strategic frontiers or on pioneer activities, supported by interested boards, societies and Churches.

The Interim Committee of the I.M.C., Wagner College, Staten Island (1954), continued the discussion of this subject :

> The urgent need for further strengthening the international and interdenominational character of the missionary movement has been expressed at this meeting in pleas for an increase in the sending of missionaries by younger Churches and the sending of international and interdenominational teams for specific tasks in certain places. The emergence of Churches in all parts of the world thus provides a God-given opportunity to broaden the base of the missionary movement, thereby demonstrating in new ways the character of the Universal Church and meeting the threat to the mission of the Church posed in certain forms of contemporary nationalism.

The Interim Committee, moreover, instructed the officers of the I.M.C. to study what is being done in the way of internationalization of missionary effort and, if possible, to start pilot projects. The subject has been discussed several times in *The International Review of Missions*. Dr. R. Pierce Beaver [2] urged the plea of the necessity of international, interdenominational and inter-racial teams. Dr. M. A. C. Warren [3] sounded a note of caution ; the title of his article, " Nationalism as an International Asset ", is in itself a warning against ecumenical romanticism.

[1] Willingen Minutes, p. 68.
[2] *The International Review of Missions*, October, 1953, p. 406.
[3] *The International Review of Missions*, October, 1955, p. 385.

Finally, recent ecumenical history has demonstrated the timeliness of this issue. I need not discuss in detail the history of the Hongkong conferences (1954 and 1955), and the Bangkok consultation (1956) leading up to the Prapat conference (1957), and the plan to found the East Asia Christian Conference. I only want to mention that according to the Bangkok findings' preamble (in the light of which the " Bangkok Plan I ", adopted in substance by the Prapat Conference, has to be read) :

> . . . there is arising in the Churches in Asia a strong sense of missionary responsibility and a compulsion to share with all Christians in the evangelization of the world. This finds immediate expression in plans for evangelization of Asia and goes together with a deep desire for the interchange of church workers among the Churches of East Asia and to internationalize the personnel working among the Churches.

And further on :

> What we have in mind is not in the nature of a new mission board or society, for we believe that the responsibility for policy decisions and the use of funds should be transferred to the Churches in Asia directly. We think rather of an Asian body which will co-ordinate the work of the Churches and missions in East Asia, stimulate their co-operation, encourage interchange between them and serve as an instrument for helping them to think through the basic issues of evangelistic policy and for the working out of a common strategy.

The importance of this quotation for our present discussion lies in the need expressed by Asian church leaders for internationalization of missionary activity. Now this may take the form either of ecumenical teams, as mentioned at the Willingen conference, or of a pool of missionaries or fraternal workers and of money, as implied in the quotation above. It seems to me that there is a notable difference between the kind of internationalization of missionary activity, the cause of which is being pleaded in these Bangkok findings, and the form envisaged at Willingen. The latter has grown up in regard to such projects as the Vellore Christian Medical College or the Makasar Theological School. In these cases it was the necessities of the work which led up to internationalization ; the co-operating boards know what project their missionaries and their money are going to be used for. Nobody will doubt the usefulness of this kind of internationalization. The Bangkok-Prapat system, however, seems to aim at internationalization, if only for its own sake ; it severs the direct relations between the sending and the receiving churches. There is no doubt that this idea can make for more efficiency and mobility. But it expects missions to renounce some real living traditions. Again, do these traditions possess an essential spiritual value, or should and could missions renounce them in accordance with the requirements of our age ?

3. *Send us no men, but money !* This is another radical thought which is in the air. It is quite normal that it should be so. The whole environment, e.g., of Asian Churches, urges them not to employ foreigners in work which nationals can do themselves ; this is the way of the independent state, why not of the autonomous church—the more so when co-operation with foreigners may be a reason for non-Christians to distrust the Church ? An Asian Christian is reported to have said at a recent ecumenical gathering : " I do not fear to look to my western brethren for financial aid. Give us the rifles, the bullets and the powder and the Asian Christians will assault the fortresses of the principalities and powers of darkness around us."

There is no doubt that this policy raises very serious issues. Is this the meaning of partnership ? Or is it right to say, even for a Christian from the west, that " the heart of the missionary movement has always been personal service. . . ."[1] And if so, does or does not the missionary situation of to-day require the missionary movement to renounce things which up till now have been their very heart ?

[1] Dr. M. A. C. Warren, *Ad Interim* Committee Minutes, I.M.C., Wagner College, 1954, p. 19.

4. *No more mission subsidies for evangelism.* An extremely
radical attitude is advocated in a paper prepared by the
American Methodist Mission, North India, " A New
Financial Policy for the New Century : [1]

> The seriousness of this particular aspect of the problem
> (viz., a mission-supported church) can be seen by two
> related factors : (1) The searching questions raised by the
> Government and others with regard to foreign-supported
> evangelism. The Government of India and our non-
> Christian neighbours seem to be saying something like this,
> " We gladly welcome generous donations to support mission
> schools and hospitals, but we strongly resent foreign money
> to support your religion, i.e., the Church. Let your Christ-
> ianity prove itself. If it is truly Indian, and the Christians
> are really what they claim to be, they will stand on their
> own feet. If not, they will fall. Let us really see what will
> happen if the foreign props are taken out from under your
> religion. Let us see if it will prove itself worthy to be
> considered a real part of India." We cannot help but feel
> that, in general, India deeply appreciates foreign help for a
> school or a hospital. It deeply resents the same help when
> it is used for the Church and particularly its evangelistic
> programme. Again we see a similar attitude in (2) the fact
> that within the Church itself the foreign-supported evangelist
> is working against great psychological difficulties. Look
> closely at the Church to-day, and it will become evident
> that the most effective evangelists are LAYMEN or MINISTERS
> WHO HAVE REFUSED TO ACCEPT FOREIGN SUBSIDY and have
> thrown themselves upon the people for their support. This
> may seem like a strong statement, but experience shows that
> when people know that an evangelist is ' mission-paid ', they
> tend to discount both him and his message. This can
> hardly help but have its effect upon the evangelist himself,
> making him aware of the barrier between him and the
> people he seeks to reach. We are aware that there are some
> glowing exceptions who are able to overcome this barrier,
> but in general it is all too true that the foreign-supported
> preacher or evangelist faces very real difficulties just because
> he is ' mission-paid '. While these attitudes arise in the
> minds of both preacher and hearer, they do not ordinarily

[1] *Revolution in Missions*, pp. 225-6.

arise in the minds of the teacher and his people, or the
doctor and his patient. Why? Because the nature of the
Christian witness is different. It is quite clear, therefore,
that it is not only proper but necessary to make distinction
between the CHURCH PER SE, and its SOCIAL INSTITUTIONS, and
to consider the support of the ministry in a different light
from the support of the institutions.

Similar questions are being asked in other countries besides
India. It is true, in the same symposium we find the Rev.
R. M. Bennett,[1] looking upon the use of mission funds as
being one out of many normal and generally accepted
relationships, such as the Colombo Plan, the United Nations'
technical assistance, etc. Why should the ' haves ' be
allowed to share with the ' have-nots ' in worldly things
and not in the Church? But even he cannot help facing
" this very real fact that financial aid from abroad and
missionary administration of it may be the largest single
cause for the spiritual lethargy so common in the Church in
India to-day."

If the things said under sections 3 and 4 are even partly
true, what is to be the future policy of mission boards?

5. *Non-professional missionaries*, i.e., those giving Christian
witness and serving the Church in secular professions overseas. The idea of non-professional missionaries is a live issue
in several countries.[2] It is certainly a good cause. Is it,
however, more than just a good cause, is it perhaps a modern
form of foreign missions? There is no doubt that this idea
too is in the air and that some, at least in the west, look upon
it as a modern form of foreign missions. I think this idea cuts
to the heart of the essential character of foreign missions as a
responsibility of the Church. Churches, or at least missions,
not individual missionaries, which send missionaries into
other countries are responsible to the Churches in the lands
to which they send the missionaries. There is an essential

---

[1] " The Church and Foreign Personnel," *Revolution in Missions*, p. 64 ff.
[2] Cf. " Oversea Service, an Experiment in Lay Responsibility," by H. B. T.
Holland, M.B., Ch.B., *The International Review of Missions*, April, 1955, p. 187.

relation between the mission's responsibility for the missionary's material position and its responsibility for his work. The older Church cannot consider as its missionaries people over whom it has no say itself and whom therefore it cannot attach to a younger Church.

Last, not least : the whole idea of the permanence of missionary relationships is disregarded as soon as people liable to transfer or dismissal by non-Church authorities are considered as missionaries.

6. *The challenge to the missionary as an evangelist.* The challenges to missionary traditions, however, do not only regard the mission's position (as those discussed above), but the nature of its work as well. What kind of work is asked of those older Churches which most conscientiously try to follow the rules of the new missionary ethics ? They are called upon to provide missionaries for branches of work such as literature production, the work of National Christian Councils, study and teaching, hospitals, etc. These are the kinds of jobs similar to those for which governments engage foreign personnel and for which secular endowment funds provide help. But am I entirely wrong in noticing a very definite trend among younger Churches in Indonesia towards seldom calling upon foreign personnel for evangelism ? Is Dr. M. A. C. Warren wrong when he says [1] :

> To-day the gravest embarrassment of the missionary societies lies in the actual unwillingness of the younger Churches to set them free to perform the tasks for which they properly exist—the pioneering of those new frontiers, not necessarily geographical, which not yet have been marked with a cross ?

Or does Prof. Paul Verghese voice the unavowed opinion of younger Church leaders when he says [2] that " the task in Asia and Africa will have to be undertaken by the small and powerless Christian Churches of those lands without much

[1] Quoted in *Revolution in Missions*, p. 167.
[2] *Revolution in Missions*, p. 180.

more aid from the west than a fellowship of prayer and concern " ?

Let us try to draw a conclusion from what has been said under this heading. The different challenges to missionary traditions, even to missionary traditions readjusted according to contemporary ethics of partnership, may be reduced to some common denominators. The least radical of them aim at de-personalization and rationalization or efficiency in the missionary enterprise of to-day. The more radical of these challenges constitute a plea that the older Churches should further the cause of evangelism in their former ' fields ' by withdrawing such financial and personal resources as are destined for evangelistic purposes. This may sound like a gross exaggeration, but it is not, if understood as what it is meant to be : an attempt at conscious formulation of an unconscious trend underlying a great number of different facts and pronouncements. This trend is there, in spite of the most sincere invitations by younger Churches to missionaries. This trend has, I am afraid, increased since Whitby, 1947, and is still increasing. If anyone asks me how I can account for the existence of this trend in the face of so many sincere pronouncements about partnership and co-operation (which I fully take at their face value and not just as expressions of ' politeness and thankfulness ') my reply will be that I am not now interested in the relation of two contradictory truths according to western concepts of logic : my problem is a problem of life, and the life of the missions of the older Churches may well depend upon the development of this trend.

4. REASONS WHY THIS TREND OFTEN REMAINS UNNOTICED

One of the reasons why this trend may easily remain unnoticed is the fact that human nature is thoroughly disinclined to notice disagreeable things and hesitates to doubt the usefulness in our days of old and venerable institutions.

Another reason is that several things serve to camouflage it from the mission boards and the older Churches. Many of our missions have work which can still go on as it used to in the nineteenth century ; there is still room for statistical data about the number of our missionaries, and for promotion and deputation work in more or less the old style. And even where missions and Churches have accepted the rules of the new missionary ethics there remain all the activities I mentioned above under section 3 (6) and which, even if they do not call western missionaries to front-line jobs, still constitute a very real contribution to the younger Churches' work.

Finally there is the world-wide inflation, also the everlasting financial troubles of missions. Are we not satisfied too easily when financial troubles have been overcome and when our mission has been able to adapt itself to the rising level of salaries and prices ? Ought not our satisfaction to be much more tempered by disappointment about a lack of requests for more missionary co-operation ? Am I wrong in supposing that if partnership in the sense of Whitby, 1947, had become anything like a reality in the unprecedented missionary possibilities of to-day in some countries, missions would be under much greater financial pressure than they are now ? All this conceals the real predicament of the older Churches' mission from our sight ; their leaders have quite enough to do along the lines mentioned above and may well dodge the most urgent question we are being asked to-day, the question *as to whether the demands of new missionary radicalism as discussed in this paper are well-founded or not.* If they are well founded, if missions have primarily to go the way of depersonalization and efficiency, maybe of withdrawal, if missions have to renounce many of their hitherto living characteristics, they might perhaps merge with I.C.A., or their organization could be at least immensely simplified. If they are not well founded, we shall want a fresh vision of the task of the foreign missionary, which in practice to a great extent means the task of the western missionary.

5. The Challenges Are Peculiar to Missions in the Ecumenical Movement

The fact, that those Christian forces which are outside the ecumenical movement and which do not recognize principles of contemporary missionary ethics of partnership are not being challenged, throws a curious sidelight on our problem. When reading publications on contemporary Roman Catholic missionary strategy one cannot help being impressed by the pushing power of this centrally led church which nevertheless knows how to integrate national desires. Its very structure prevents it from being challenged the way ' our ' (I.M.C. and W.C.C.) missions and Churches are. The same applies to the other extreme on the ecclesiastical scene : to faith missions and sects, where there is no room for any central leadership and missionary comity and very little for national leadership in the younger Church. Of the 24,000 American missionaries of to-day, 58 per cent belong to boards which are not, and 42 per cent to those which are in the Division of Foreign Missions, N.C.C.C. in the U.S.A., and this percentage has been growing. Even if we know that the importance of the co-operation of an older Church cannot be expressed in its number of missionaries, these figures give the impression of the great evangelistic pushing power of faith missions and sects. Are we sure that Churches and missions in the I.M.C. equal them in this respect ? In any case it is right to say that only Churches and missions which are in the ecumenical movement and therefore recognize the younger Churches' " absolute spiritual equality and . . . right to manage their own affairs . . ." (Whitby, 1947), are being challenged as described above. There seems to be a vital relationship between the ecumenical disposition of our missions and the challenges to their missionary activity. If this is true, ought we not so to review our missionary ethics that the older Churches in the I.M.C. and W.C.C. may enjoy a greater freedom for missionary activity with no brakes applied by some of their very best friends ?

T.G.A.—7

A considerable readjustment in the older Churches was necessary when ' their ' mission work took the contemporary form of partnership.   This shift has been entirely wholesome to the missionary thinking of our generation.   However, I confess my inability to see how to put the challenges of the new radicalism before the older Churches and still to keep their allegiance to the cause of missions thus understood.   I fear that even the least radical of these challenges will make these Churches feel that some essential spiritual values have been lost.   I would find it hard to prove that they are wrong, but I am willing to learn.   Even a short reflection about the promotional consequences of the new radicalism shows that there are much deeper problems at stake than just the income of the mission boards.

6. Our Response ?

What is to be our response to these challenges ?   We have first seriously to consider whether missions ought not to renounce some of their traditions referred to, take I.C.A. form and take a considerable decrease of income into the bargain.   This may be partly compensated for by a decrease of cost in home activities.   Another possibility would be for foreign mission boards to turn into home missions.   Indeed, the challenges referred to above would not hold good in the home country.   And we know that there are no ' Christian ' as opposed to ' non-Christian ' countries.

In either of these cases foreign missions, as the world has known them, would come to an end.   There is no reason why it might not be their duty to accept this.   Foreign missions developed their present form under circumstances greatly different from those prevailing now.   It might well be their Lord's will for them to follow the law of the grain of wheat : unless it " falls into the earth and dies, it remains alone ; but if it dies it bears much fruit ".

All this would not be necessary if the new radical trends did not after all, either in theory or in practice, express what is in the minds and the hearts of those upon whom the shape of missionary policy-to-come depends. It might then imply for missions what I called earlier in this paper " a full realization of partnership, a new vision of the place of their missionaries in the accomplishment of the world-wide task of evangelism, a form of service, which does justice to the essential freedom of the spiritual vocation, a fresh possibility ' to burn out for God ' ".

I do not see what is the way of obedience to God's will in this issue. Let us hope and pray that the Ghana Assembly of the I.M.C. may shed some light upon what He wants missions to do, being preserved both from conservatism and from radicalism for their own sake. Missions, like all human organizations, may well outlive their usefulness, but should not, on the other hand, be dispensed with lightly.

Humanly speaking, the question is of paramount importance for the cause foreign missions have stood for. Unless missions catch a new vision of their task, the days of their partnership and co-operation in the lands of their present-day activity will be numbered, even if they keep alive for quite a considerable time. We must not let their still intact position in some parts of the world and the useful things they are doing everywhere allow us to dodge this issue.

October, 1957.

III
SELECTED SPEECHES DELIVERED AT THE ASSEMBLY

THE CHRISTIAN MISSION AT THIS HOUR

By

JOHN A. MACKAY

The Chairman's Address to the Assembly

I HAVE been asked to introduce to your attention the chief subject of concern that has brought us to Ghana, and which will constitute the main theme of our deliberations during the days we spend together. *The Christian Mission at this hour*—this is the topic of my address and the theme of the Assembly.

Let me begin by asking, What do we understand by ' this hour ' ? How do we interpret the ' Christian mission ' in such a time ? It is a permanent Christian obligation, and one enjoined by Jesus Christ Himself, that Christians should ' discern ' the particular time in which their lot is cast. Such ' discernment ' can be exercised in two ways : first, in terms of *historical perspective*, and second, in terms of *apocalyptic significance*.

As regards the *historical perspective* in which the Ghana Assembly is set, this is the first occasion on which a meeting of the International Missionary Council takes place in Africa. This in itself is important. We assemble, moreover, in the territory of one of the two youngest nations in the world. The only nation still younger is Malaya. Ghana is a country which symbolizes in a glorious way the steadily growing importance of the Negro race ; it is the harbinger of an era which lies beyond the tragic tensions of the present hour.

There are familiar faces, however, that we miss. No delegates from China are here, although last week in Hungary I met Chinese fellow Christians who were visiting the Protestant Churches of that country. This is part of our tragic situation. In certain regions of the globe, alas, Christians cannot confer to-day with fellow Christians, who are the fruit of their missionary labours because the nations to which they respectively belong are bitterly estranged from one another.

Certain other facts, also, are worthy of attention as we approach our theme. A world so closely united by technology that space and time have been transcended is, at this hour, so divided by suspicion and hate that universal discord is regnant. Those of us who come from the west are poignantly aware that the prestige of the western world has been rapidly declining and that the white man's sovereignty is being boldly challenged. Yet at the very time when no missionaries can enter certain countries in Asia, we have the joy of knowing that in those same lands vigorous new Churches, which are both national and autonomous, bear witness to Christ and the Gospel.

When we take a closer look at the life of mankind to-day we realize that this is an *apocalyptic hour*. It is an hour weighted with destiny, an hour when the elemental forces of human nature and history are laid bare, and when a titanic struggle is in process to determine the type of human individual who shall populate the world of to-morrow. Let us ask this question : Where exactly do the hands now stand on the clock of time, and what is the inner spiritual meaning of ' this hour ' in the history of the Christian Church and the destiny of the human race ?

We are living in what the Bible calls " a day of the Lord ", a day of darkness rather than of light. Yet our time is one of God's springtimes, albeit, one of His terrible springtimes. It is like that springtime which the prophet Jeremiah saw in his youth on the Judaean plateau near his home in Anathoth (Jer. i, 11, 13). Gazing at a spray of wild almond, the first shrub in the land of Judah to show signs of life at winter's close, the young prophet became vividly aware of God's quiet awakeness. But he saw something else also. In the background he saw a boiling cauldron set on glowing embers that were fanned by a northern breeze. The sizzling pot was a symbol of an approaching attack from Israel's enemies in the North country. But this is the important thing : the green spray, the symbol of divine mercy, and the fuming vessel, the symbol of divine judgment, were equally a part of God's springtime awakeness.

We cannot escape the fact that while we meet in this lovely place " darkness covers the earth and gross darkness the people ". This is another phase of our tragic situation. The road which millions and millions of our fellow men and women travel to-day finds them literally on " a journey through Dread ", unlit by any illumination from above. They are pilgrims in a world without values, in which self-interest, expediency and compromise are the sole absolutes. In international relations, the current trend is to reduce every problem to a scientific problem, to a problem of technological achievement, or of military might. More urgency is shown in getting a mechanical gadget into the sky than in sitting down to talk quietly with estranged fellow humans on earth. Men are more interested in soaring into interplanetary space than in crossing the frontiers and barriers that separate groups and nations on this terrestrial globe. The new planetary, interdependent world, which technology has created, is rifted by hate. Yet its creator is utterly helpless to solve the problem of human alienation.

In the meantime, men become increasingly depersonalized, even dehumanized, and live in deadly peril of becoming pure robots. More and more they have to fight to maintain their position as individual human beings. Very apt is the title of a recent book by a contemporary French thinker, Gabriel Marcel, entitled, *Men Against Humanity*. The individual person is being lost in the human race. There is something more : a spirit of conformity, a morbid quest of security, and a general lack of enthusiasm and conviction have become the order of the day in wide sectors of society, especially in the west.

How very far the process of secularization has advanced since the Jerusalem meeting of this Council in 1928 ! Some of us were present at the unforgettable sessions on the Mount of Olives. A famous paper was prepared for that gathering entitled " Secular Civilization and the Christian Task ". It was brought home to us that the thought of our generation was being emptied of religious ultimates. To-day it is not merely that God is rejected amid the general eclipse of the Divine. A state of mind prevails which is more radical than traditional atheism, the mere rejection of God. The whole human order, as we have known it for centuries, is being challenged and rejected. " I don't accept God's world," says a character in Dostoevski, speaking prophetically for very many of our contemporaries. " I return to God the entrance ticket of existence."

But in this attitude of revolt there is a strange, hidden hope, a beam of God's springtime, that pierces the contemporary gloom. There is being sounded a fresh call to courage and commitment, even on the part of those who deny God and read Him out of the universe. If man is to be man, it is said, if life is to be liveable, if mankind is to have any future whatever, men must create their own values and commit themselves to them with passionate devotion. It is being recognized by men like the Frenchman, Jean-Paul Sartre, that in a situation like ours to-day there is no alternative to commitment and a sense of mission. So it is not surprising that new absolutes begin to appear which have a strange aura of religion around them. Some of those absolutes are purely cultural, some, such as nationalism, are political in character.

Still another element in our present-day situation must be noted. In parts of the western world both the Christian and the Greco-Roman tradition recede into the past. As Hendrik Kraemer, with prophetic insight, emphasizes, we are headed for the first world-embracing encounter of cultural ultimates. Speaking more concretely, we are witnessing in secular circles the birth of a strange new kind of religious consciousness. Why is this so ? Because secularized man, being still man, cannot divest himself of an ancient human tendency to absolutize, and to create for himself idols towards which he takes up an attitude of religious devotion. In the meantime, ancient religions, which had been thought dead or moribund, have suddenly become resurgent and have taken on new life. As a result of this, Christianity, Christians, and the Christian Church are now headed for the greatest spiritual encounter with the non-Christian religions since the days of the Roman emperor, Constantine. Thus it is, that, though it may be expressed to-day in very novel and unconventional ways, there begins to appear in the soul of contemporary man an intense God hunger, and a new sense of the need of mission.

In such a situation, and at such a time, the question takes on new meaning : " What is the Christian mission at this hour ? " Let me attempt to answer the question. The time is clearly ripe to probe deeply into the theology of *mission* ; it is no longer enough to raise questions regarding the policy of *missions*. This basic question confronts us : What does *mission—mission of any kind*—mean ? What does it signify to have a sense of mission ?

Mission, it may be said, is the dedication of life to promote something which is regarded as having supreme value. A sense of mission may be born within an individual or a group in one of two ways. It may have its origin in an experience of inner compulsion, or it may be derived from the voluntary acceptance in a feeling of being called to action, of a mandate which is issued by a recognized superior authority. In each case where a sense of mission is real, an individual, or a group, becomes the willing and devoted servant of a task which has been accepted, whether that task be to embody an idea, to be loyal to a cause, or to give allegiance to a person. Where mission becomes real, men are the joyous and obedient servants of something which they regard as bigger and more important than themselves, whether that something be a great idea, a great cause, or a great Being. Let me go further and say : *A sense of mission is not only an important historical or physiological phenomenon in the lives of men, it is of the very essence of life itself.* Men become truly alive when they know who they are and what they stand for.

If this is what mission signifies, if mission and servant are inseparably conjoined, what is meant by *Christian* mission ? Christian mission is the voluntary and joyous dedication of life to promote an idea or a cause which is inseparable from loyalty to Jesus Christ, who is Himself both the Truth and the Life.

We are now ready to explore the theme of *the Christian Mission at this hour.* There is in the Christian religion what may be described as the Mission Quadrilateral which has four closely related but clearly distinguishable aspects. The four constituent aspects of the Christian mission are these : (1) the mission of the Christian faith ; (2) the mission of the Christian man ; (3) the mission of the Christian group ; (4) the mission of the Christian Church. Let us consider these in turn.

1. THE MISSION OF THE CHRISTIAN FAITH

If a discussion of the Christian faith and its mission is to be realistic and relevant, it must be undertaken to-day in an entirely new context. This context is a new manifestation of the religious consciousness of mankind, or at least of a fresh interest in religion. Here is the strange paradoxical fact. In a world which, according to every appearance, is thoroughly committed to secularism, it is being recognized that the religious consciousness of man is both a universal and a potent fact. Men tend to think and live religiously, even when they pursue purely secular ends. In Communist ruled countries, for example, those in authority are forced to recognize that religion is no mere opiate which was injected into people by sinister social groups who were interested in their enserfment. It has become clear that religion is a

dynamic force, which even a Communist government must
take into account, a force which it must conciliate, and,
where possible, use for its own purposes. We, therefore,
have the paradox of Communist rulers becoming the patrons
of religion.

What is still more striking, however, is the current revival
of the old religions to which I have already referred. Buddhism is becoming a markedly dynamic force in Ceylon.
Hinduism is resurgent in India. In this great continent of
Africa a new defence of Animism is being undertaken and,
in consequence, a fresh sanctity is being attached to many
ancient customs which were in process of disintegration. The
resurgence of these old religions is closely related to nationalism. New significance is being given to everything belonging
to the heritage of a people.

These ancient faiths, moreover, are developing a sense of
mission and becoming missionary ; some of them, like
Hinduism, are becoming missionary for the first time in
their history. In many instances they are even changing
traditional emphases in order to become more relevant to
the cultural mood of to-day, and especially in order to meet
the demands of the new nationalism to which each becomes
related. Among intellectuals in particular a new interest
in the old faiths is developing. Not long ago the Hindu
philosopher, Radakrishnan, boasted that " eastern religions
aim at producing heroes and saints ; western, men that are
sensible and happy."

The new awakening of man's religious consciousness in
our secularized era, and the resurgence of the old religions
are closely related to the quest of freedom. This is natural,
for the fundamental notion of religion is freedom. Buddhism
offers freedom from existence. Hinduism offers freedom from
unreality. A new brand of religion in western countries
offers freedom from futility. Christianity offers freedom
from the bondage of sin, as guilt and self-centredness. The
belief that some desired form of freedom can be attained
through religion underlies the reborn interest in religion on

the part of many people, who in former generations would not properly be called religious. Putting the matter in another way, religion and God are being subtly used by contemporary man to promote his own interests, or the interests of his nation. In every instance, the particular form of religion to which men have recourse in their quest for freedom is derived from some particular perception of reality. In all religious commitment an ultimate perception of choice is always involved.

This brings us immediately to Christian faith and its mission. Here, too, an ultimate choice has to be made, a primal decision has to be taken. The question is asked : Who or what is God ? Is God merely the highest value ? For some forms of religion God is just that, and religion consists in devotion to the highest value or to the ultimate truth. But in the Christian religion God is not the highest value or the ultimate truth ; He is rather the source of all truth and value. He is a Living God who speaks and acts, a God who entered, in human form, into the time process to save men from their sinful self-centredness. By reconciling men to Himself and to one another, through death and resurrection, God makes them His servants to build a community called the Church, whose mission it is to proclaim the Good News of God and prepare the way for the coming of His everlasting Kingdom of righteousness and peace.

Thus Christianity takes its departure from the perception and affirmation of a living, speaking, and acting Deity who Himself engages in mission. The God of the Christian religion is a missionary God.

An insight of that great Frenchman, Pascal, into the core of the Christian religion, which came to him in a profound religious experience, is very timely and relevant in the situation which confronts Christianity to-day. For Pascal, the ultimate reality which confronts man is not an Idea God, " not the God of philosophers or savants ", but a God who entered into history, the God of Abraham, Isaac, and Jacob, the God of Jesus Christ, the God who won the personal loyalty of that great scientist, philosopher, and saint and became his God forever.

There is a Christian thinker of our time, an Anglican layman, H. A. Hodges, who re-echoes the thought of Pascal in very similar terms, and says :

> I shall contend that Christian thinking proceeds on a pre-supposition of its own which I shall call *the Abrahamic presupposition*, or *Abrahamic theism*. For the New Testament insists over and over again that Abraham is the model for Jew and Christian alike and that the true Christian is the spiritual child of Abraham, that is, one whose attitude towards God is the same as Abraham's was. . . .
>
> Abraham is the story of a man who has committed himself unconditionally into the hands of God ; a man who does what God asks of him without hesitation, however para-doxical or self-contradictory it may seem, and who accepts God's promises however mysterious and incredible they may appear. It is by virtue of this unconditional self-commit-ment to God that he has won the title of the friend of God.

Here is a crucial fact about which we must be quite clear. The starting-point of the Christian faith is not a reflective idea regarding Deity, nor a haunting sense of the Divine, nor a passionate devotion to some ultimate value, but a response to God, who disclosed Himself redemptively in the history of a people, the children of Abraham, with whom He entered into covenant, and who finally revealed Himself in a Person, Jesus Christ, in whom He became incarnate.

In the Christian faith God's missionary movement towards man culminates in a Person. It is no exaggeration to say that *Christianity is Christ*. " Our message is Jesus Christ. He is the revelation of what God is and of what man through Him may become." This affirmation was made thirty years ago at the meeting of this Council, held on the Mount of Olives. It is in Christ that the true nature and mission of both God and man are revealed. Here is the glory and, at the same time, the scandal of the Christian religion. The God of our faith and of the Christian mission is a God who showed Himself to be an extrovert, whose nature as love became manifest by the fact that He *so* loved that He gave His Son, His own very selfhood. God came into history, not as a celestial summer tourist interested in the aesthetic, or as a playwright who staged a tragic drama, or as a judge and avenger of the deep-dyed sins of man. He came to be involved in man's humanity. In human flesh He died for human sin, and rose again from the dead and ascended into Heaven to reconcile all things to Himself.

The story of what God did for men in Christ and can do to-day in men, who through faith commit themselves to Christ, is the Gospel, the *Kerygma*. This Gospel of the action of God in Christ, incarnate, crucified, risen, and coming again, is to be proclaimed to all men everywhere. This is the *mission* of the Christian faith. What is proclaimed in this Gospel is not a true doctrine or a sound principle, but a Person who is Himself the Truth. The great objective of the Gospel's proclamation is, in full loyalty to the express commission of Jesus Christ Himself, " to make disciples of all nations ", or as it might also be expressed, to restore wholeness to a broken humanity.

The salvation of men, which it is the mission of the Christian faith to accomplish through the Gospel, can best be described in terms of the restoration of human beings to holiness of life, that is, to wholeness in their lives. Men who are saved recover likeness to God, receive the filial spirit of the sons of God, and voluntarily and joyously dedicate themselves to the service of God, thus becoming God's servants. To unify once again the divided kingdom of man, so that God may become King in the lives of men individually and corporately is the goal of the Christian Gospel and the mission of the Christian faith.

The full rich meaning of Christian mission is most luminously and adequately communicated by means of a classical but forgotten biblical image. I refer to the *image of the servant*. The servant image, I have no hesitation in saying, is the essential image of the Christian religion. It is the image which sheds the truest light upon the mission which God set for Himself in history. It is the image which illumines the mission of Israel as a people. It is the image which lights up the mission of Jesus Christ Himself, as well as the mission of Christians, both individually and collectively.

In the Old Testament, prophets, priests, and kings are called God's servants. They do His will and carry out His purposes. Israel as a people was to fulfil its destiny under God by being God's 'servant'. We read in Isaiah, " He said to me, ' You are my servant, Israel, in whom I will be glorified . . . I will give you as a light to the nations, that my salvation may reach to the end of the earth ' " (Isa. xlix, 3, 6).

In the New Testament the servant image offers the most adequate interpretative principle for the incarnation of God in Jesus Christ. In the thought of St. Paul in his letter to the Philippians, " Christ Jesus, who though He was in the form of God, did not think equality with God a thing to be grasped, but emptied Himself, *taking the form of a servant*." The Son of God became the servant of God in order that He might fulfil the mission of God. Throughout His entire earthly life, Christ's strong sense of sonship with God moved Him to act joyously as the servant of God. He knew that He was one with the Father, and that He bore the Father's likeness, yet He said, " The Son of Man came not to be served, but to serve, and give His life as a ransom for many." In the Upper Room, the night in which He was betrayed, Jesus had a vivid awareness " that the Father had given all things into his hands ". He knew that His hands were regal hands, to which the sceptre of universal dominion belonged by right. Nevertheless He borrowed a towel and did a servant's menial act. Jesus was intensely conscious that He had " come from God and was going to God ". He knew that His lot was set by nature in the orbit of Deity. Nevertheless He moved towards humanity in the " form of a servant " to wash and dry the grimy feet of His astonished disciples. He thereby performed an act which was associated in the minds of His followers with that of an oriental slave.

It was to fulfil the mission of the " suffering servant of the Lord " that Jesus Christ handed Himself over to His enemies and died upon the Cross, from which He continues to reign. It was because Paul, Christianity's greatest convert, accepted the lordship of the crucified, risen, and ascended Christ as worthy of his utter allegiance that he begins his great letter to the Romans with these words : " Paul, a *servant* of Jesus Christ, called to be an apostle, set apart for the Gospel of God ". The servant image may well be called, as indeed it has been called, a ' bridge category '. It serves to unveil the inmost nature and glowing passion of a God who in order to fulfil a mission took the " form of a servant ". This same image also provides a pattern and a norm whereby individual Christians, missionary societies, and the Christian Church as a whole may learn how to fulfil their God-given mission.

II. THE MISSION OF THE CHRISTIAN MAN

The Christian mission must primarily, and even ultimately, be expressed by individual Christians. There can be no substitute for personal witness.

What does it mean to be a Christian man ? What does it signify to be a man at all in any real sense ? When is man truly man ? Man is truly man when he is God's man. He begins to fulfil his human destiny, when he commits his life to God, when God becomes his God, and he voluntarily and joyously becomes God's ' captive ', God's servant. This is said with due regard to the sad fact that there are hosts of Christians who betray the Christian faith.

But when all is said, and full penitence is expressed, Christians are nevertheless the only people who can achieve manhood and womanhood in the deepest, truest sense. In New Testament language they have been called to be ' saints ', that is, to be God's men and women. They constitute a " new creation in Christ Jesus ". Christ becomes the Lord of their life. They became His friends. They give proof of their friendship with Christ by doing His will, exulting in His service, joyously taking the form of servants.

The world-wide community of Christians to-day has no greater need than that everyone who bears the Christian name should be a Christian in truth and develop a sense of mission. The Christian mission can never be fulfilled in this era, unless Christians take their relationship to Jesus Christ and His Church with the same seriousness that people, who are not Christians, take membership in the secular group to which they belong. Very often, unhappily, we Christians who belong to the traditional denominations, both in the older and the younger Churches, do not compare favourably in the quality of our Christian devotion with members of the so-called ' sects ' whom we are apt to despise. How often we look down our ecclesiastical noses at those fellow Christians with an air of superiority and disdain. But let us face the sobering New Testament fact. All Christians are called to be ' saints ', and should take their calling seriously. Otherwise it will go ill with the Christian mission at this hour.

But if Christians are called to be ' saints ' in this profoundly New Testament sense, what does it mean for them to engage in mission? Every Christian should be a witness to his faith at all times, in all circumstances, and in every environment. He must seek every opportunity to bring men into allegiance to Christ. For that reason *he must have an intelligent grasp of his faith.* He must take seriously what St. Peter enjoined. " Always be prepared to make a defence to anyone who calls you to account for the hope that is in you . . ." (1 Peter iii, 15). He must have a simple working theology. He must also feel in his heart the inner constraint of Christ's passion for men. This love passion, through which Christ continues His work, uses a Christian man as an instrument, a medium, a servant, whereby it becomes communicated to other people.

The Christian in the fulfilment of his mission must also identify himself closely with the people to whom he bears witness and with their environment. By the way in which he makes himself a sharer in their life, with all its problems and sorrows, he will win a right to be heard. His strategy of identification, however, will involve neither an air of condescension in dealing with other people, nor an uncritical conformity to the kind of life they live. His aim will be to restore human brokenness, and to create spiritual wholeness. For the salvation which is the supreme objective of the Christian mission is spiritual health, the restoration of true humanity in the lives of men and women.

Never, however, can the Christian mission as here described be carried on effectively unless two conditions are fulfilled. First, the Christian laity must realize that they are called to an apostolate. Second, those who are professional servants of Christ and His Church, those in a word who are the contemporary equivalent and successors of the New Testament " apostles, prophets, evangelists, pastors, and teachers ", must realize and take seriously that their supreme task in the Church is, as Paul puts it in his letter to the Ephesians, " to equip the saints for serving " (Eph. iv, 12), that is, to make them true ' servants ' of Jesus Christ.

Ours is the era of the laity. Only lay men and women, by living lives that are utterly Christian in every secular vocation, in government and diplomacy, in industry and commerce, in the home and in the classroom, in the clinic and on the farm, can do what Christianity needs to do in our time to fulfil its mission.

III. THE MISSION OF THE CHRISTIAN GROUP

It is natural for Christians to group together, both as an expression of the essentially social character of human nature, and in order, as members of a responsible fellowship, to accomplish some goal they have in common. From the origins of Christianity to the present there have always been

T.G.A.—8

the " two or three gathered together " in the name of Christ, to whom Christ assured His presence. Some of the greatest movements in Christian history have been born in fellowships of this kind. In fact, in the history of the Christian Church, great new visions and crusading zeal have almost always been born in small groups of dedicated Christian people.

It was thus that the great missionary societies of the nineteenth century came into being. Missionary-minded people banded themselves together. They formed a society to secure and commission men and women for some missionary task, or to go to some mission field themselves. All too often official Church bodies have been more interested and successful in achieving *order* than they have been in creating and sponsoring *ardour*. They have tended, in fact, to be suspicious of ardent spirits. Men and women of Christian vision and zeal have not infrequently found it difficult to fulfil their ideals of mission under the official sponsorship of the ecclesiastical organization to which they belonged. Hence, the independent missionary society.

Here is a fact which this Assembly cannot ignore. Some of the most famous of missionary societies in the Protestant tradition, and some that have been most loyal to the International Missionary Council, and at the same time most creative in facing human needs on the great frontiers of the Kingdom, have been, and continue to be, independent of the Churches to which their members belong. I still recall how startled I was when I learned that none of the dozen or so societies organized by Anglicans to achieve some practical goal to which the members of the particular society are dedicated, are officially related to, or controlled by, the Church of England. The same situation has obtained in very many Churches in continental Europe. The largest and most famous of European missionary societies have not been Church-inspired or directed.

On the American continent to-day, independent missionary societies are much more numerous than those officially connected with Churches. They also send many more missionaries into the *Oikoumene* than do the Church-related missionary organizations. The reasons for this development are complex. In some instances those organizations have quite unfortunately lacked a sense of the Church ; in others they have lacked confidence in the dedication of the Church to mission. There has also been a fear that ecclesiastical control might stifle Christian initiative. Cases are not lacking in which outstanding young men and women of good education and dedicated lives have preferred to go into missionary service under the auspices of an independent or ' faith mission ', rather than relate themselves to a traditional Church mission board. They are afraid, especially in the new era of the ' fraternal worker ' and in view of the demand for specialized technicians, that they will have to sacrifice evangelistic opportunities. On the other hand, many of those ardent missionary spirits withdraw from the real world where their lot is cast and so become quite irrelevant to it.

There are, on the other hand, some notable cases, of organized denominations, in which the Church is literally the mission. This is true of the Mormon Church. It is no less true of the Pentecostal Churches. In many parts of the world to-day every member of the several Churches that make up the Pentecostal World Fellowship are not only committed Christians, but ardent missionaries. Thanks to Pentecostal zeal, the government of Chile. recently paid a tribute to the tremendous social transformations which had been wrought in the Chilean Republic as a consequence of Pentecostal religious effort.

It is all too easy to think disdainfully and speak disparagingly of independent missionary societies, of ' faith missions ', and the rest. Many of these groups are accused of being unco-operative, and of showing themselves hostile to the ecumenical movement. In very many cases such missions do not form part of the National Christian Councils represented in this Assembly. There is a growing trend, moreover, for many of those societies to become integrated into a parallel organization. This should give us great concern.

Some reflections are therefore in order. In the Roman Catholic Communion, the many religious orders which carry on missionary activity in different parts of the world do so with full autonomy, and do not function under the direction or direct control of the Vatican or of the Roman Catholic authorities in any given country. It was a startling revelation, to which Protestant Church leaders in the United States awoke some years ago, when it was discovered that the representatives of Roman Catholic missionary societies in America were convening for the first time in their history. It seemed incredible that in a great monolithic structure, such as the Roman Catholic Church, the Church's missionary work should have been carried on by independent Roman Catholic orders, whose representatives had never met together to co-ordinate their work or to think through a common policy.

Think also of the monolithic political structure of all Communist states. Nevertheless, within a given state, the Communist party itself functions autonomously and independently of the government as such. The party, as a matter of fact, while not being directly controlled by the government in power, is the chief force that inspires and directs governmental policy.

Thought will be given at this Assembly to co-ordinating and intensifying the world mission of the Church. The question will be asked whether the traditional missionary movement as represented by the International Missionary Council should become more closely related to the World Council of Churches, the world body which represents the Churches as such and with which the International Missionary Council has been ' in association ' since 1948. It is of the utmost importance that we gain the needed perspective and ponder all relevant facts, in order that the Christian world mission in our time may be advanced and that every lesson, which may be profitably learned from missionary effort past and present, may be turned to good account.

Certain things are clear. First, no achievement of

ecclesiastical order through the fulfilment of all the great proprieties of Christian relationship as between foreigners and nationals, between native pastors and fraternal workers, can ever be a substitute for missionary ardour. Whenever a constituted Church body becomes indifferent to the Church's mission, a problem is created for those interested in mission. Wise counsel will then be needed, if full justice is to be done to the proprieties of ecclesiastical order, on the one hand, and to the demands of missionary ardour on the other.

Second, the Churches and Councils which belong to the official ecumenical movement should not regard as necessarily unecumenical those missionary societies and Churches which have thus far been unco-operative in the co-ordination of missionary effort in given areas of the world. Every possible effort should be made to treat the members of those societies as brethren in Christ, to seek opportunities to meet them and to learn from them, and also to disabuse their minds of certain very erroneous views which they hold with regard to the ecumenical movement, the Churches and Councils which support the International Missionary Council, and the World Council of Churches.

Third, a way must be found whereby missionary societies which have a traditional fear of ecclesiastical control in their missionary work, or who believe that Church bodies as such can never carry on worthy missionary activity, should find a place in whatever plan is adopted to integrate the historic missionary movement into a structure which represents the Churches as such. It would appear that patterns and experience are not lacking to ensure the full independence of any given missionary group which relates itself to the International Missionary Council and to the ecumenical movement as a whole. On the other hand, we in this Assembly should see to it that the insight, zeal and autonomy of such bodies are welcomed and cherished within the corporate expression of ecumenical unity. In this way a united front in the name of Christ and His Church will be presented to all Christianity's rivals in the world of to-day.

IV. THE MISSION OF THE CHRISTIAN CHURCH

We come now to the Church as such and to its mission.
But what is the Church ?

Definitions abound as to the Church's nature. Many of
these definitions are rich and meaningful. Whatever more
the Church may be, it is at least this, *the community of those
for whom Jesus Christ is Lord.* The Church is community
before it becomes organization. To-day the Christian community is world-wide. Groups of Christian believers are
found in every nation on the globe.

With more insistence and relevance than ever, the word
sounds, *Let the Church be the Church.* When these words
gripped me more than two decades ago, I wrote down this
comment which I recently uncovered among some old
papers. I would re-echo the same sentiments to-day.

> Let the Church *know* herself, whose she is and what she
> is. Discerning clearly her own status as the community of
> grace, the organ of God's redemptive purpose for mankind,
> she must, by a process of the most merciless self-scrutiny,
> become what God intended her to be. Nothing less than
> that, nor yet anything more than that. In penitence and
> in humility must the Church rediscover the meaning and
> implications of that word that comes to her from the earlier
> ages of her own history, " to be to the Eternal Goodness
> what his own hand is to a man ". This involves a revivified
> sense of God as a real living God, the " God of the whole
> earth " over against a God who is a mere idea, or a dialectical
> process, or a member of a polytheistic pluralism. This means
> concretely that the Church recognizes herself to be the
> Church of Christ, the organ of God's purpose in Him. It
> must be her ceaseless concern to rid herself from all sub-
> jugation to a prevailing culture, an economic system, a
> social type, or a political order. Let the Church live ; over
> against all these let the Church stand.

In those days the term ' ecumenical ', which to-day is so
current, was just emerging. Now we begin to speak about
' ecumenics ' as the new science of the ecumenical. What
does ecumenics mean ? Ecumenics I would define as : *the*

science of the Church Universal, conceived as a world missionary community, its nature, its mission, its relations, and its strategy. The given in this young emergent science is the Christian Church as " a world missionary community ".

For the first time in history the Christian Church, as a result of the Christian missionary movement, can be spoken of as a world community, that is to say, a community which is found in token form around the globe. The contemporary task of the Church is to assure that wherever members of this community are found, they shall be missionary in word and work. It cannot be emphasized too much or too often that *mission* is of the *essence* of the Church. It is the chief glory and goal of the Church's earthly unity that it should be a united front for missionary action. Such action should take place on all the frontiers of the world, and not merely the geographical frontiers ; for every sphere where men live and work and suffer is an appropriate frontier for the Church's missionary effort.

The most luminous and dynamic figure with which to describe the mission of the Church is once again the servant image. It was the true destiny of Israel, the covenant people of God, as we have already seen, to accept her rôle as God's servant in order to become " a light to the nations " and carry God's salvation " to the ends of the earth ". The Christian Church, amid all the diversities of her structural form, and underlying all the ecclesiological theories that seek to define her nature, is inescapably, as Paul said, the " new Israel ". Being such, it is the Church's mission to be God's servant, his envoy, at this hour, to enlighten and disciple the nations of the world, and to lead all men everywhere into the community of Jesus Christ. Therefore, " Let the Church be the Church ! " Let the Church in our time take the " form of a servant ". Let it give fresh, dynamic, missionary significance to this classical Biblical image which needs to be recovered and redefined in our time.

But, alas, in many ecclesiastical circles it is thought scandalous that the Church should be thought of as a servant. The servant rôle and emphasis is regarded as derogatory to the dignity and status of the Church. Is not the Church the people of the Covenant ? Yes, but too often the Church has gloried in her status as the *people of God* and has been too little concerned about being the *servant of God*. Pardon the irreverence : but too many Church people and Churches as a whole have, so to speak, chummed up with Deity. They have become God's supercilious patrons instead of His loving friends and His obedient servants. Friendship with God has been regarded too frequently as a treasured experience, a high distinction to be cultivated for its own sake. Sufficient regard has not been paid to the fact that Abraham, the classical pattern of friendship with God, embarked at the call of God upon a supreme adventure ; that the Son of God exultingly took the " form of a servant " ; and that Jesus affirmed categorically that His true friends are those who do what He commands them.

It is painful to think in how many respects, and in how many places, the Christian Church is becoming an absolute, an idol, an end in itself, without regard to its true nature and honourable mission as the servant of Jesus Christ. Yet, let there be no mistake about this, no claim to be the Church, no historical continuity, no unbroken tradition, no apostolic succession, no theological orthodoxy, no ecclesiastical unity, no political power, no liturgical pageantry, can be a substitute for the Church's missionary consecration, in the form of a servant, to the redemptive purpose of God in Christ.

And as regards those Churches which we call ' younger ', no degree of autonomy, no measure of harmony, no attainment of all the requisites of self-government and self-support, can guarantee, still less be a substitute for, a Church's dedication to her missionary task. The truth is this : the moment the Christian Church in any of its determinations begins to glory in anything that it is, or claims to be, and neglects to fulfil its mission in the form of a servant, this could happen. The Church of to-day as an organized structure could meet the fate of the ark and the temple in ancient Israel. It could go the way of the old Jerusalem and God would raise up out of the ruins " new children unto Abraham ".

No, literally nothing that can be said about the Church, or claimed by the Church, will be of any ultimate avail if the Church neglects to fulfil its God-given mission. The Church's structure and doctrine, her liturgy and even her sacraments, fulfil their highest function, and express their deepest meaning, when they prepare the people of God to be the servants of God. The breaking of bread in the Upper Room at the Holy Supper, the Eucharistic Feast, was followed directly by the washing of feet, when our Lord took the form of a servant. Never let us forget the deeply symbolical significance of this fact. The servant image must be restored in our time. In the comradeship of the Church universal as a world missionary community, the older and the younger Churches must catch the vision of the servant and assume the servant form. The Church must become afresh a pilgrim Church and engage in a new Abrahamic adventure. It must beware of identifying itself too closely with any culture or with any nation. It must not be ashamed to have elements of strangeness in the eyes of its contemporaries and be foreign to the standards of the world.

The pilgrim Church, on its Abrahamic missionary adventure into the *oikoumene*, will seek to fulfil a three-fold mission.

First. In every society and in every age the Christian Church has a prophetic mission to fulfil. To be true to its mission the Church must radiate the light of God upon the world. It must set the life of man in the light of God. It must recognize that God is One and that He is interested in every phase of human life and welfare. It must proclaim that Jesus Christ is Lord, over the world and over the Church and over the souls of individual persons.

The Church is called to a prophetic ministry in contemporary society. Those Churches which are powerful and free in the nations where they bear their witness are particularly called upon to exercise a prophetic ministry. Let them proclaim to nations that take up a purely negative attitude towards Communism and seek to meet the Communist peril exclusively in terms of missiles and military preparedness, that God is the sovereign Lord of all things. He, who in the ancient days of Israel's history used Assyria, Babylon, and Persia for the fulfiment of his purpose to be the " rod of his anger " and, perchance, to be his ' shepherd ', can use Communist states in the life of to-day for the same end. The problem of contemporary history and of human destiny is much more complex and lies much more under the judgment of God than appears to many naïve and shallow statesmen, who control the destiny of great nations to-day.

Let the Church proclaim that in human relations, even among enemies, there can be no substitute for personal conference. Let the Church shout aloud that civilization, and all the nations that consider themselves to be civilized, stand in need of forgiveness. Let the Church make unmistakably clear that even in international affairs, and despite the long record of failure around the conference table, there is still a place for the injunction of Jesus regarding a quality of patience and of forbearance in human relations which involves a ' second mile ' and the ' seventy times seven ' of forgiveness.

The fulfilment of the Church's prophetic mission is closely related to a true theology, which should be at once Biblical, dynamic, and relevant to the thought problems of the hour. In this connection, literally nothing has happened in recent years that gives greater hope for the development of a true theology in the lands of the younger Churches than the gift which was announced this morning by Dr. Charles Ranson. Under the guiding light of the Holy Spirit, this gift can bring a new dawn in the development of theological education, and contribute to the preparation of a prophetic ministry for the Church Universal.[1]

[1] This refers to a gift of $4,000,000 for the development of theological education in the lands of the younger Churches. Two million dollars were contributed by Mr. John D. Rockefeller, Jr., and two million by eight mission boards in the U.S.A.

Second. The Christian Church has likewise a redemptive mission to fulfil. This mission consists in mediating the love of God to the world. The Church carries forward the mission which God Himself initiated when the Son of God took the form of a servant. This is the mission in which God the Holy Spirit is still engaged in the world, and which He carries forward through the instrumentality of the Christian Church as the Body of Christ.

In the fulfilment of its redemptive mission, the Church must communicate to all men with both passionate conviction and crystalline clarity, the Gospel of the love of God in Christ Jesus. The proclamation of the Gospel, however, must be more than mere talk. It must be communicated by deed as well as by word. No one can be an effective Christian witness if he is a mere talker. The Christian Church must make manifest the meaning and spirit of the Christian Gospel. Through the mediation of the divine love to meet human need, it must proclaim its message in ways which are related to the true welfare of men. The word must continue to ' become flesh '. The Church must be so sympathetic to everything truly human in the life and culture of a people that all that is good in their cultural heritage may be preserved and transfigured. The Church to-day must seek to do in many lands what Christianity succeeded in doing many centuries ago when it preserved what was best in the cultural heritage of Greece and Rome.

Finally, *the Christian Church has a unitive mission to fulfil.* It must seek to achieve and express that kind of unity which should mark the people of God, the servants of Christ, in the fulfilment of their mission to the world. Let the Church never forget that the true pattern of her unity is that oneness which exists between the Father and the Son. That divine unity, let us remember, the unity which marks the life of the Holy Trinity, is not a static, but a dynamic unity. The unity that exists in the Godhead, I say it with reverence, is a missionary unity. Father, Son, and Holy Spirit are together dedicated to a missionary task, and the unity of the Church becomes effective in the measure in which the world believes that the Father sent the Son to be its Saviour and so takes seriously the Christian message of redemption.

Therefore, in loyalty to God's revelation of Himself as Father, Son, and Holy Spirit, and in holy dedication to God's missionary task, let Christians and the Christian Churches become " partners in obedience " and " fellow workers with God ", that the world may be saved in the fullest Christian sense.

Let us never forget this : it is on the road of missionary obedience that the unity of the Church of Christ will be achieved and will prove most effective. It is on this road, and only on this road, that a pilgrim, missionary Church, which subordinates everything in its heritage to the fulfilment of its mission, will discover the structural form and appropriate organ which will best express its oneness in Christ and contribute most to its missionary service for Christ. On the road of the Church's missionary obedience the Holy Spirit will reveal the form of ecumenical organization which is most in harmony with the reality of the Church as a world community which seeks to be loyal to its mission and its unity.

To that end, " let the leaders take the lead ". Let them lead in such loyalty to the great Biblical tradition and to the spirit of Christ, that they and the Churches which they serve shall become servants of all. For the Christian Church will never be so truly the Church of Christ, and never so relevant to the needs of this generation, as when it takes the " form of a servant ", even of a " suffering servant ". Let the Church of Christ in every land be willing to endure persecution and to risk ridicule as it serves God and men, inspired by the deathless hope that the kingdoms of this world shall one day become the " Kingdom of our God and of His Christ ".

My brethren, may the work of this Assembly at Ghana equip us all, and the Christian Councils which we represent, to advance *the Christian Mission at this hour*.

28th December, 1957.

THE CHRISTIAN MISSION IN ASIA TO-DAY

By

U KYAW THAN

A Speech delivered in Plenary Session in the Assembly

INTRODUCTION

As I stand here I wish again that Bishop Manikam had decided early enough to attend the Assembly for the planners of the programme to use him for this presentation and that I in my wanderings to and fro, and with my limited background, had not been asked to introduce the topic which he formerly would have been approached to present. This is no complaint, but a confession of my inexperience and an acknowledgment of the fact that I am very much a novice and a layman not deeply exercised in the consideration of the great issues, which must engage the spirit and the mind of the Assembly at this time.

Perhaps what I might say, either in my enthusiasm or in my inexperience, may serve as somewhat provocative starting-points for the Assembly to touch up the incomplete sketches or to tone down the colours where they are unnecessarily glaring. These comments can only form an introduction to the work of the groups, which may each fill up the gaps or develop debates on the type of issues indicated, according to the merits and deserts of each case, and also add more relevant and significant subject-matter for each session. Without attempting to expound abstract theories or principles involved in the Christian mission in Asia to-day, I hope simply to pick out a few factual situations and, as it were, to think out loud on some issues which emerge from the consideration of such situations. If in this task I

sometimes draw heavily on my Burmese background, I hope
it will be understood that it is not because I feel the Burmese
situation to be predominantly important, but because it will
help me to be concrete and specific.

Asia to-day is an object of immense interest to the outside
world and to us Asians ourselves. It is easier to develop a
spirited discussion on Asia than to talk about *positive* action
on the Christian mission in Asia to-day. Some may feel
that as it so often leads to frustration and blind alleys, it is
better to dismiss, out of Christian charity, the controversial
issues or to avoid them altogether.

" The pattern of Christian mission must change ", is what
everybody seems to say. But the mission boards, or their
equivalents, have their technical difficulties to overcome in
their structure and operations. The boards may be eager
to adjust, but the contributing members cannot be told the
whole story about what is happening in the missionary
enterprise. It might mean killing one's father by hammer-
ing away the bee on his head, or throwing the baby out
along with the bath-water. While this may be very interesting, it cannot be our starting-point. We have, then,
already taken for granted that there is something to be
perpetuated, though we do not seem to be quite agreed on
what it is. We then begin with the presupposition that there
is, in the good sense of the word, a vested interest, which must
in any event come out on the right side. Since the Christian
mission is much larger than missions as such, it would be
unfair to become completely preoccupied with missions
every time we talk about the Christian mission in Asia,
Africa or Latin America. At the same time, without being
preoccupied only with missions as such, it should be possible,
in considering " the Christian mission in Asia ", to limit
our thoughts, for the present purpose, to the matter of the
proclamation of Christ to the unchurched or to the witness
of the Church to those outside her life, rather than taking up
everything that can possibly be included under the title,
" the Christian mission in Asia to-day ".

ASIAN RENAISSANCE

In talking about Asia to-day people are generally excited about and taken up by the revolution that is going on. The wave of renewed nationalism, the attainment of sovereignty by the Asian nations and the social and economic experiments, along with their implications, usually dominate the analysis and assessment of Asia, by Asians and non-Asians alike.

While we may all be fascinated by the Asian revolution, there is an intangible but consequently more important factor which people either tend to forget or to which they pay only lip-service, in analysing Asia. Not long after the war, Dr. Nambara, a former president of Tokyo Imperial University, was underlining the importance of the ' Renaissance ' in Asia in his addresses to students and educators, as he looked forward to the reconstruction of the educational system in post-war Japan. This fact of the renaissance in Asia is much more important than the revolution in Asia, for it was the renaissance that raised up the revolution and was in turn accentuated in its fruits or manifestations by the revolution. The reassertion of traditional values, the redefinition of culture and society and the emphasis on the *selfhood* of Asian nations are, after all, products and also manifestations of this renaissance in Asia. Without going into the crystallization of all of them, I will dwell only on the resurgence of ancient religions in Asia. There is a general tendency among some Christians, both in Asia and abroad, to pay lip-service to this resurgence. In Burma some Christian workers who do not know a sentence of the classical language, ' Pali ', and who could not understand a profound book in Burmese, and have not really listened to the expositions during the Buddhist council sessions, and therefore cannot understand wholly the significance of the ' resurgence ' of Buddhism in Burma, dispense with it by concluding that it was a nationalistic and at best a cultural revival. It cannot be denied that the political revolution had reinforced and further strengthened the renaissance. Since Buddhism and Burmese culture are bound up together, the renaissance in Burma implies the revival of culture there. But beyond the level of the political and the cultural, there is also the initial ' renewal ' at a still deeper level which, for lack of a better term, may be called ' theological '.

If one were to take a plane and fly to Rangoon, an interesting sight, as the plane approached the airport, would be the great Buddhist pagoda or shrine, covered from top to bottom with gold, glittering in the sun. According to tradition, the origins of the shrine date back to the sixth century B.C. Two merchants from Burma went across to India during the lifetime of Buddha and, having met and heard the preaching of Buddha, pleaded with him to favour them with some memorable and visible relics to carry back to Burma as reminders of the singular privilege and opportunity they had been granted. The head is the glory of the person, and Buddha gave them four threads of his hair, which were enshrined in the great pagoda at Rangoon. The first Buddhist council was held after the demise of Buddha in 544 B.C., and since then from time to time, when occasion required, Buddhist councils were held to ensure that his teachings were kept and passed on to successive generations in their original purity. There are fifteen canonical books in Buddhist scriptures, and for each of the canonical books there are eight standard types of exegetical works. Hence a Buddhist theologian would normally be expected to know not only the fifteen canonical books but also the 120 exegetical works.

In A.D. 1057 there was something like a reformation in Buddhism in Burma. The most recent council, the sixth Buddhist council held at Rangoon, was in direct descent from the great councils held since the sixth century before Christ. For all these 2,500 years Buddhism had undergirded Burmese culture and society. All this is mentioned simply to emphasize one point : the Christian missionary enterprise in Asia, except possibly in Japan, has often missed out one great challenge. If you read the memoirs of Adoniram Judson, the great missionary to Burma in the nineteenth century, and study the daily entries in his diary in 1819 and the aspirations which he then had, it is rather uncomfortable to see how neglected some of those original aspirations are in missionary work in Burma to-day. Judson was eager and unflinching in his efforts to learn the Burmese language and to study the Buddhist scriptures and Pali. He struggled to proclaim Christ among the Buddhists. Later missionary efforts went, it is to be feared, in the direction where the going was good. The hill tribes and the less developed people were easier to win over, hence the majority of the Christians in Burma are drawn from among the hill tribes. The real presentation of the Gospel among those people who form the majority in Burma and many of whom, instead of looking up, rather look down upon the enthusiastic and not necessarily satisfying presentations of the Gospel by the average missionary—yes, among this majority of the Burmans the real presentation of the Gospel had not happened as far as one can see. Therefore, even though we can count up to 138 years of missionary work (if we count only from those days of the visible impact starting from the witness and life of Judson), the significant phase of the evangelization of Burma and the Burmese people had hardly begun. For the evangelization of Burma in this sense would mean taking seriously the challenges and opportunities of the Christian mission among the Buddhists, taking seriously the resurgence of Buddhism, not merely in terms of its social and cultural implications, but in terms of its theological significance for the Christian mission.

For lack of a better formulation, I would borrow, with all its limitations, the phrase, the theological penetration of the Buddhist system, and this it seems to me is the urgent and ongoing need in the task of evangelism in Burma. The missionary from non-Asian lands often moves among certain groups, such as the ignorant and the handicapped. He is ready to spiritualize the physical and material needs of those with whom he gets into touch. It is, I suppose, true that often there is no real encounter between persons. There is also no meeting of mind with mind. For the people whom he meets tend to become objects for aid or assistance and the relationship is between that of the object and the subject ; and what Martin Buber describes as the relation between ' I and Thou ', the sustained encounter between the Christian and the Buddhist, seldom developed. The Gospel is either irrelevant or a folly to the Buddhist, not because the Buddhist has understood the Biblical meaning of the ' scandal ' of the Cross, but because the proclamation of the Gospel has, for him, not really happened. While on the one hand the Gospel is not being really proclaimed among these people, with their rich and refined philosophical traditions, their resurgent religions are now beginning to publish their claims for universal validity and relevance. They had claimed it from the very early days. But this claim is now asserted with a new conviction and vigour, in the context of the weaknesses and shortcomings of the so-called Christian nations.

In concluding this section, I want briefly to register a few remarks. One concerns the Institutes for the study of the living faiths of man in Asia. In one Asian country I know, the whole purpose of the work seemed to mean just teaching the foreign missionaries in a foreign language the elementary content of the religion concerned. While we must acknowledge the usefulness and place of such labours, let us not mistake the branch for the tree-trunk. Unless the study and labours are undertaken within the framework of the original language, thought-forms and actual Christian people of the land, there are going to be new barriers and new problems to be tackled in Christian missions amid the Asian renaissance to-day. I would also remark, though I do so with fear and trembling, hoping that the spirit in which I speak will not be misunderstood, that while we have in Asia an extremely limited number of people who could help us with this task, and while we need all the resources and available help to multiply and intensify the knowledge and work of these people, they are being taken away from us (to translate from the Burmese saying) to fill the pot which seems to us to be full. I want here to re-emphasize the need, now as never before, theologically to disentangle the confusion between the west, western culture and Christianity. It often seems that, for the Buddhist, Christianity implies the social and cultural categories of the west, and not always at their fundamental best. A cultured Buddhist or Hindu, unlike the man from the bush, will therefore wonder why he or she should give up altogether the rich heritage and the long-standing refinements for the sake of some other culture and heritage, even if these could be proved temporarily useful. Fundamentally, the task of the Christian Mission in renascent Asia is a theological one, and I rejoice at the announcement of the possibilities regarding the fund for theological education.

I hope I have not laboured too much an example for considering the mission of the Church in the Asian renaissance. While in the significant realm of ideas, thought and religious values, the re-awakening of the mind is taking place in Asia, the Church can witness to supplement this *awakening of the mind* with the *quickening of the spirit* in Asia for the redemption of the nations in our part of the world.

REVOLUTION IN ASIA

Having said these things, which to me are more important than preoccupation with the political revolution in Asia, I must nevertheless dwell for a moment on the Asian revolution. In spite of all that ecumenical gatherings and Asian Churches are saying, there is still much misgiving about the relation between Christianity and power politics. I need not repeat the worn-out references to the unfortunate historical coincidences, not only between the missionary

advance and the political expansion of western powers, but
also between missionary withdrawals and the retreats of
western régimes. I am thinking of the establishment of the
Communist régime in China and of the exodus of the
western missionaries from that great land. I can also think
of the Japanese invasion of Burma and the departure of
these missionaries from Burma, or of the capitulation of
Japan and the influx of foreign Christian workers into that
country, or in Taiwan. I say nothing about the reasons
and circumstances in which they decide to come or go. I
am only registering the facts of history and the confusion
in the minds of non-Christians in forming their opinion of
the Christian Mission in Asia. These have not helped
either the Churches or the missions in their witness to
Jesus Christ. From the point of view of the local church
the western missionary can be interpreted as one who is
there only when the skies are clear. The missionary may
say that his departure is for the safety of the Christian
community about to face hardships and for his own family's
sake. But in all humility I have often wondered whether
these are the best Christian reasons. There, I think, we may
still have much to learn from the Roman Catholic Fathers.
I am not thinking of their celibacy but, rather, of their
pastoral commitment in a different way. Many non-
Roman Catholic missionaries from abroad are often citizens
of two worlds—the world of their own mission boards and
the Churches back in their own countries, and the world
of the Churches to which they are sent and of which they
are often guests or consultants rather than committed
members sharing the same discipline.

As the Asian countries regain independence or re-establish
their sovereignty, new limitations are being placed by the
governments on the execution of the traditional missionary
enterprise, partly because of the confusion and misgivings
mentioned earlier. There is also a new emphasis in the
Christian Mission in Asia to-day in underlining *diakonia*
during our time. While I have no doubt about the validity

of the approach from *diakonia*, I fear there are other developments in which the Christian mission is thought of almost in terms of a watered-down technical assistance programme flying a Christian flag. There is a possible danger in the tendency to become too much fascinated with the approach from sociology, anthropology, psycho-analysis, group dynamics and audio-visual aids ; so much so that while the Churches in Asia need to grapple with the fundamental theological issues of our times in our own contexts, the questionable remedy is offered in terms of the debatable diagnosis.

Perhaps a point which arose out of recent conversations with M. M. Thomas, of India, may indicate in a better way what I am feeling after here. There was a time, in parts of many countries in Asia, when missions were moralizing and civilizing agencies. They were pioneers bringing morality and civilization to the communities in Asia through western educational institutions, moral instruction, hospitals and social service programmes. Now, there are moral giants outside the Church to whom non-Christians can point. Gandhiji, Vinoba Bhave and national saints and stalwarts among the priests, philosophers and leaders may be quoted with conviction by such contenders. Realms of service which were formerly the pioneering fields for the Christian missions are now occupied by the Welfare State, with its movements and programme of national uplift and reform. Is the Church in fulfilling her mission to be a city set on a hill *or* the leaven in the lump and the salt seasoning the earth ? Perhaps the Church's fulfilment of her mission may lie in the direction of the attempt to define and proclaim the ' redemptive ', as she participates in these programmes and movements, rather than grudgingly and defensively sticking to her compounds. I have used the words ' *perhaps* ' and ' *may lie in the direction of* '. I do not want to absolutize the implications of the thought. The key point at issue is that *now* as never before God is calling the Church to proclaim the message of justification by faith over against that of justification by works. Until Christ is acknowledged and accepted as Saviour, all human works and programme will be dogged by the element of the tragic and frustrating. In Him are the good news and the glad tidings amid the revolution and reconstruction. If the wholeness of the apostolate and the inter-relatedness of the proclamation, fellowship and service are present in the Christian mission, I believe again the good news in Christ will be heard afresh and accepted in Asia, Africa and everywhere.

THE COMMON EVANGELISTIC TASK IN ASIA

My final section is a summarized reflection on the significance of the East Asia Christian Conference which it is proposed shall be set up as an instrument of co-operation among the Churches and Christian Councils in Asia in the desire to undertake their common evangelistic task. The report of the East Asia Christian Conference, held at Prapat, Indonesia, in March, 1957, is available and I will not go into the history of the development of these desires in East Asia, especially from the time of the meeting of the I.M.C. at Tambaram, India, in 1938, through the first post-war East Asia Christian Conference in 1949 in Thailand, the establishment of the Asia Council on Oecumenical Mission, with the support of some Churches in Asia to further the task of Christian mission in Asia, the I.M.C.–W.C.C. Consultation at Bangkok in March, 1956, and the subsequent coming together of all but six of the member Churches of the W.C.C. and the member councils of the I.M.C. in East Asia at Prapat in 1957.

In March, 1956, the I.M.C. and the W.C.C. called a consultation at Bangkok, Thailand. . . . The Consultation was attended by the officers of the Asia Council on Oecumenical Mission, the general secretaries of the two world bodies, the East Asia Secretary and other consultants from Asia and some executives of the mission boards related to the Asia

Council on Oecumenical Mission. The Consultation declared : " *One of the most impressive and hopeful developments in the Christian situation* in Asia, which we owe in no small measure to the work of the first East Asia Secretary of the I.M.C.-W.C.C., is that there is arising in the Churches of Asia a strong sense of missionary responsibility, a compulsion to share with all Christians in the evangelization of the world. This finds immediate expression in plans for the evangelization of Asia, and is marked by a deep desire for an interchange of church workers and to internationalize the personnel working among the Churches. We recognize the contribution that Churches elsewhere must continue to make, but we share a common conviction that the world-wide mission of the church is the responsibility of Christians everywhere.[1]

" We feel strongly that we must find ways and means to enable our Churches to discharge their responsibility and to fulfil this truly ecumenical desire. The future of evangelism in Asia must surely be a co-operative evangelism in which all share with each other for the common good, and in which we manifest increasingly our ecumenical unity. What we have in mind is not in the nature of a new mission board or society, for we believe that the responsibility for policy decisions and the use of funds should be transferred to the Asian churches directly. We think rather of an Asian body which will co-ordinate the work of the Churches and Missions in East Asia, stimulate their co-operation, encourage interchange between them, and serve as an instrument for helping them to think through the basic issues of evangelistic policy and for the working out of a common strategy.

" Our starting-point is the East Asia Secretariat. This has fulfilled a very important function in bringing the churches and councils in East Asia more closely together. But the time has now come to give it a wider mandate and strengthen it in personnel.

" We therefore request the I.M.C.-W.C.C. to call a representative conference of the member Churches of the W.C.C. and the member councils of the I.M.C. in East Asia to

[1] In this and following paragraphs, use is made of material contributed by the author to *The Common Evangelistic Task* (Papers and Minutes of the East Asia Christian Conference, Prapat.)

consider how the new task which we see before us may best be fulfilled."

It was proposed that the functions of the East Asia Secretariat of the I.M.C. and W.C.C. should be enlarged to include a survey of the mission of the Church in East Asia and of the available resources of personnel and funds for its fulfilment, consultation among the Churches in the area and missionary societies, promotion of the participation of the Asian Churches and councils in the programme of the two world bodies, mutual sharing of experience, information and personnel among Asian Churches and assistance in interpreting and co-ordinating the programme of ecumenical inter-church aid in East Asia.

> The conference was also convened [the report goes on] at a time when the two world bodies, viz., the World Council of Churches and the International Missionary Council, were seriously confronted with the question of integration. Prapat conference conclusions on the need to develop a regional instrument which would serve the total mission of the whole Church in the area, and the emphasis of the conference on the inseparable relationship between the various manifestations of the apostolate indicated the urgency of the challenge to the two world bodies dealing with the related aspects of Christian mission to come together within an integrated framework. The pressure of the world, with its social and political developments and the basic pressure of the Word of God as felt by the Christians in East Asia, implied there was no further possibility for the ' Churches ' as such and the ' Missions ' as such to operate in isolation from each other. The mission in a given land must be felt and carried out as the mission primarily of the Church placed by God in that land. Surely the need for co-operation and the bearing of one another's burdens across regions and continents remained. But the Christian congregations and communities, namely, the Church of God placed in a given land, must learn to render her own obedience to her Lord who was seeking to gather His people in every land.

The mission is the mission of the Church. While the

statement is accepted generally, there is no real clarity yet about its meaning for those in Asia. The mission of the Church—yes. But, in a given country, the mission of which part of the Church Universal ? The mission of the receiving Church or of the sending Church ? Sometimes there seems to be an emphasis even in the sending country on the mission of the mission board, rather than of the Church to which the board is related. In the receiving country the mission seems to be the mission of anybody except that of the Church in the country concerned. I think we still need to take more seriously the challenge to manifest the mission of the Church in its integrated form both at the local and at the national level, be it in the lands of Asia, Africa, Latin America or the rest of the world. I submit that while mission is of the essence of the Church, in Asia we must also pray that God be manifested as the God of order and not of confusion. If Christians are members and organs of the same body, they must function as organs of the healthy body—the body of Christ—and not as those of a paralytic man.

Ultimately it means a re-dedication of our purpose, a renewed vision of the Church and the *waiting upon God* in the light of His word so that we may be obedient to His will if perchance He would make us His instruments in His purpose of offering Christ the Saviour to the world.

This will also mean humility if in His purpose of building His temple it pleases Him to choose Solomon rather than David. There is no reason for David to be possessive of God's purpose.

And, having done all, it may be that we must recognize that we have done what lies in us in rendering our obedience, but recognizing that we are after all still unprofitable servants, until the Master in His mercy grant us His grace and blessings in His Kingdom.

30th December, 1957.

CHANGES IN THE PATTERNS OF WESTERN MISSIONS

By

W. FREYTAG

A speech delivered in Plenary Session in the Assembly

THIRTY years have passed since the Jerusalem meeting of
the I.M.C. in 1928. It would be instructive to work out
similarities and differences between that meeting and ours.
At first glance there appears to be a repetition of main
themes and subjects. I remember quite well what then
seemed to me to be the most important points of the Jerusalem meeting. There were three. The discussion about
our message confronting the non-Christian religions, the
new impetus to take up the social problems in Asia and
Africa and the strong representation of those who then were
labelled younger Churches. This time, if we take the
subjects of our groups as parallel to the main themes at
Jerusalem, the witness to non-Christian religions and in
society comes up again, but in an entirely different context.
These themes appear to be entirely—so to say—taken in
and swallowed by the third point which was at Jerusalem
not so much a theme but a fact, the younger Churches.
And if you look at other themes of our groups : the place
and function of the missionary ; the meaning of ' partnership ', then you get at the main point of difference between
then and now. Then missions had problems, but they were
not a problem themselves. There was no question that the
initiative in witness and action was with western missions
as they stood. To-day we do not speak of the initiative of
western missions but only of their contribution. But more
than this : we are uncertain about their patterns as they

are and even more, the historic, basic conceptions of missions are being questioned. Let us state at the very beginning : it is no question at all that there is no Christian life, no living with Christ without a missionary task. But the question is whether our present patterns of carrying out that task and the conceptions behind such patterns are the right expression of the obedience God wants from us to-day.

1. FACTS

The facts which have brought about the change of situation and which raise the questions are familiar. I name three of the new realities.

There is the fact of rising nations creating new political and cultural situations. Many countries have acquired a new political status and many others are striving for it. There is a deep national self-consciousness in many parts of the world. It wants equality of cultural status, education and development, but at the same time it is looking for ' our own way '. It has a deep longing for self-realization on the basis of its own spiritual and religious heritage. This new political reality is still unstable in many instances— there are many ' not yets '—and these are particularly sensitive against all influences from outside.

There is the reality of the younger Churches. The most moving experience in visiting them is to realize how they are felt by Christians as their own. Naturally they take part in the development of their nations, striving as Churches, too, to a status of equality, and to find their own way of expressing their faith ; and they, too, show the sensitiveness of all young life. They need help. But they have begun their task of being the Church and of carrying the Gospel to their own people and even farther.

And there is the third reality, the ecumenical era. There is a new kind of togetherness in this world : the drawing together of nations in *blocs* : the use of the same vocabulary all over the world, albeit with very different meanings : the rising of a kind of secular mission ; the spreading of religions, transgressing their traditional boundaries. All this is happening so suddenly. And at the same time the new forms of togetherness of Christians : in the World Council of Churches, the confessional world bodies, the growing Christian world agencies with special tasks, none of which can be world organizations without reaching out into all the world and without making their constituencies conscious of their being a part of a world-wide fellowship and awakening their responsibility for it.

These facts have influenced the patterns of western missions in a different degree according to the different stage of development of the Churches and the areas concerned, but some general tendencies may be indicated.

The first is limitation. The sphere of work of western missions is becoming limited.

There are the closed and closing doors. We do not forget China and we are aware of increasing difficulties in quite a number of countries to secure entry-permits for western missionaries. But of more general importance is the limitation which restricts us because we are western missions. The political and cultural situation in many countries in itself means fewer western missionaries and self-limitation in many respects. We have not only to avoid unnecessary offence but to avoid labelling the Gospel as something western, as being in contradiction to the ardently desired ' own way '—what mission would not sympathize with this desire ! In so far as resurgent religions are regarded by many nationals as a spiritual backbone for a still unstable unity of the nation, the western missionary as such stands in the way of the Gospel being understood.

Another limitation is put to us by the existence and the growing self-responsibility of younger Churches. That again means fewer and fewer missionaries. Who would want to impede the development of Churches which in some degree depends on the absence of missionaries ? In China I have seen many tokens of the grateful remembrance of missionaries, but on the other hand there was an un-deniable satisfaction in the new self-consciousness that the Churches have gained by being themselves alone respon-sible. In other countries I found missionaries who decided to return home because they thought it best for the develop-ment of the Church. But if we do not go so far, at least there is a certain limitation of the initiative of the western missionary. These Churches have to find their own way. We cannot do it for them.

And there is the limitation conditioned in the ecumenical era in the broader and narrower sense of the word. Closed doors in some countries may lead in others to the multiplica-tion of newly arrived missionary societies. How often it is that such multiplication has disturbed a sound missionary policy of a society which hitherto was the only one in that area. The many forms of co-operation which become more and more necessary restrict the freedom of self-expression of the individual missionary society. Co-operation does not always prove to be an enrichment : it often means a levelling down.

The second change of patterns may be characterized under the catchword ' the lost directness '.

On account of the situation you have an inescapable growing of branches of missionary work, necessary and legitimate branches, which tend to develop a kind of exuberance. Or you have the fact that the help the Churches need means increasingly material and financial help and less personal help. In co-operation more and more contributions are necessary which carry less and less a direct, permanent share of the giver. Such contributions may be of a great value but you pay and pray, and it is over and done with. The lost directness effects a growing uncertainty in the planning of western societies. For instances, they have to be prepared to help and train missionaries. But in many instances the specialists the younger Churches want cannot be trained and stored in order to have them in case they are wanted. There are

many such uncertainties.   And with quite a number of
leaders of western societies you get the impression that in
spite of all their commitment and activity, they feel as if
they are moving in a fog.

The loss of directness is largely found among western
missionaries who are serving in and under younger Churches.
Because the initiative cannot be their own, there is a wide-
spread feeling of frustration.   In one Asian country I found
more missionaries who expressed in confidence this frustration than those who had found their way.   There was no
undue pretension behind it.   They simply could not bear
the loss of directness I am talking about.

The third change you may call the ' endangered image ',
the loss of that conception of ourselves which guides us
consciously or, even more, unconsciously.   Notice that I
am speaking not of the Mission in a general sense but of
western missionary societies in their empirical shape.   They
began by sending missionaries.   In some countries missionaries were trained and sent out even before there were any
missionary societies.   Now we see that Mission does not
consist in missionaries only.

The societies have sent missionaries to proclaim the
Gospel in order to bring about what had happened in the
times of revival out of which the societies arose, that people
might turn to Christ, that they might be converted to Him.
Now this aim is submerged by much missionary work
which is only indirectly connected with it.

The societies regarded themselves as groups of true
believers and their service as a vicarious service for what
the Church should do.   Now there is much missionary
consciousness in many Churches, and if the Churches are
conscious of the fact that missionary obligation is of the
essence of the Church, what, then, of the conception of a
vicarious service of missionary societies ?   The societies
pray for missionary younger Churches, but what, then, of
the conception of the particular group as essential for the
fulfilling of the missionary task ?

For a long time the societies have been unique in their work, in the sense that they were almost the only bridges for the service to foreign people. This was the reason why they gathered among their supporters many who felt a mere social responsibility to foreign people and not a specifically missionary one. Now that uniqueness is no more. They have their activity among many other activities, which are missionary in some sense, but in very different expressions. That means that many people who share the sense of the missionary responsibility of the Church do not find the way to share the work of the societies.

All these changes are not only the concern of western missions. Their problems in a certain respect are problems of the mission of the Church as such. I am thinking not only in terms of the missionary strength of Christianity which largely depends on the future of western missions. I think of the fact that the younger Churches cannot conceive of mission without imitating western missions, in a positive or a negative way. In both cases there is the danger that roads are built in the wrong direction.

2. REACTIONS

But now, what are the reactions of western missions ? There are different possibilities. The first one is the ordinary human reaction of just remaining passive. There are many excuses for it. Is it not, to mention only one of them, at this moment sometimes the more responsible way, not to restrict ourselves, and to do what a certain younger Church is apparently not able to do ; to insist on more missionaries where the man-power of a younger Church is not sufficient to provide the necessary pastoral service ? But the responsibility of the moment may result in a permanent weakness of the Church concerned, and all such excuses easily turn into a mere self-assertion.

There is the second possibility—the attempt to escape. We try to escape back to the beginning, looking for new unevangelized fields. As a matter of course there are legitimate tasks, but if the guiding motive is to escape the situation of service in and with the younger Churches, it may be disobedience to take them up. There is a kind of escapism which goes in the opposite direction, not backward but ahead, into projects and new plans which seem to be a step forward, but in fact are flight.

And there is the last possibility. The attitude of obedience, which takes the situation and tries to learn the lesson that God gives us. I indicate three lines only.

1. We have to accept the facts and give up any defensive attitude. It is the same danger in missions as in the Churches. We are again and again tempted to identify our empirical, human and therefore imperfect realization, in this case the Church as it is, the mission as it is, with the Church we believe in, with the mission of the Church. What was a historic expression of genuine obedience in its time becomes an entity in itself, separated from the character of obedience, and stands in the way of a fresh and new expression of the same obedience which is now asked of us. The very beginning of new obedience is conditioned in the giving up of old images which we have had hitherto and which God apparently takes away from us.

2. Another obstacle in finding the way is the human resistance to acting according to our insights. To learn means to take decisions. Ideas, even acknowledged principles, are not yet decisions. If, for instance, we were to take seriously our insight that the younger Churches cannot answer the word of God in foreign forms of thinking and expression, we should cease to send missionaries and teachers and theologians almost untrained for understanding the spiritual tradition of the special area in which they serve, and we should really take up the task which lies behind the younger Church study and which may render a great service, greater than we imagine. We all know there are other acknowledged principles of even greater importance, especially in the realm of co-operation and

unity, which have not yet become decisions. They are like clouds which stop us seeing the way God wants us to follow.

3. In all the facts there is a clear lead towards concentration. I am not going to discuss priorities. I think of concentration in the deeper sense in which by way of the changing situation God, so to speak, concentrates us. There are situations in which we still have the opportunity to proclaim the Gospel in the midst of resurgent religions which, to a certain degree, have taken up ideals and ideas rooted in Christianity but cut off from their roots, Christian ideas without Christ. There the humanistic overtones which our message used to contain have become dangerous and are sometimes obstacles to our message. Does God not make us free for the more difficult but essential task, to concentrate on the message of Christ Himself, which means on the message of the Cross ? In some states there is the tendency for the state to take over and to monopolize some activities which have been classic branches of missionary work : educational, medical, philanthropic work. I remember the word of a leading Chinese Christian who, when we passed a former missionary institution, said : " Fortunately we are liberated from them now." This was not grim humour, not only remembrance of the time of the tax burden under which the Churches almost broke down ; there was more behind that remark, a genuine feeling of a new beginning at the centre of the task. I hope it is not necessary to translate it into the situation of western missions. In many of the facts which we characterized as limitations of the western mission, particularly what we indicated as limitations in the ecumenical era, we find new openings towards the centre secretly hidden. We do not find them if we do not try to follow what God is doing step by step.

3. THE CENTRAL TASK

But what is the central task ? I cannot develop a theology of mission, but I will try a few lines, and even these cannot be more than preliminary words, mostly dotted lines.

T.G.A.—10

Mission means taking part in the action of God, in fulfilling His plan for the coming of His Kingdom by bringing about obedience of the faith in Jesus Christ our Lord among the nations.

In that context missions as empirical organizations or institutions (there is no obedience possible without becoming concrete in such human form) are one indispensable member in the varieties of services of the Churches.

Their task consists in being sent to proclaim the Gospel outside the Church, to gather into one the children of God who are scattered abroad (John xi, 52). (We should not forget the centripetal conception of mission which the Old Testament has in common with the New.)

That means that this service has to remind every Church that it cannot be the Church in limiting itself within its own area, that it is called to take part in the responsibility of God's outgoing into the whole world, that it has the Gospel because it is meant for the nations of the earth, and that the Church has its life towards that end, the goal of God in the coming again of Christ.

That means that this service consists in the sending of witnesses and all that may carry the Gospel from church to non-church. This service of missions is human service, it cannot claim to be exclusively the mission of God. It has its time and is subject to the relativity of all human service.

But the mission of God is more. It does not consist in our taking part, but they who live in the obedience of faith are part of His action. May I tell you of a recent experience I had in China? It looks like a digression, but it is not. In Peking I was asked to give a report about the Church in Western Germany. I answered : " I do not like such a general subject, give me a concrete theme : what is it exactly that you want?" Twenty-four hours later the Faculty gave me the theme : " How has the Church in Western Germany since 1945 given witness to the Lordship of Christ over this world?" That at first sight looked like compelling the western guest to produce self-criticism before an eastern audience. But I am certain that this was not the intention. They wanted something else, the model, the picture of how another Church is doing what they themselves want to do. I think the evidence of Christian decision, Christian living and Christian action is the main missionary service without which all other missionary undertakings are vain. It is an illustration only of what I said, that they who live in the obedience of faith are part of God's action. An illustration only, not the matter itself. This fact, that every Christian is a part of God's action towards His goal, has a much deeper meaning.

If we speak about God's action, God's mission, then we touch a secret greater than we are able to perceive, exactly the secret which is mentioned in Colossians iii, " Your life is hid with Christ in God ", and in 2 Timothy ii, when Paul the prisoner writes : " I endure everything for the sake of the elect ", meaning that by his suffering he is furthering the mission. The decisions of God's action are made in our life with Christ. There, more than the decision about our personal destiny takes place. There it happens that the Holy Temple of God is being built to its consummation. It happens or it does not happen, therefore according to how we live with Christ or do not live with Christ, we are a part of God's mission or we stand in its way. Therefore a Christian life cannot be lived without the wide horizon, the view of the world which God has in mind, the world which God loves. There God's mission is going on and it will be disclosed at the Day of our Lord.

30th December, 1957.

A SPEECH BY DR. KWAME NKRUMAH, PRIME MINISTER OF GHANA

Delivered at a Garden Party to Members of the Assembly of the I.M.C. and Others

Mr. Chairman, Fellow Christians :

It gives me great pleasure to address you on this occasion of the first meeting of the International Missionary Assembly in Accra, the capital of Ghana, in this first year of our independence. On behalf of the people of Ghana, I welcome you to our country, and I pray that God may guide your deliberations and make your conference and your stay here in Ghana really rewarding and worthwhile.

There are indeed special reasons for welcoming to this country a conference such as yours. Ghana is glad and proud to pay its tribute to the great work of missionaries in West Africa. If you have time to visit more widely in this country, you will often find as you travel along the roads, little cemeteries lost in the bush where lie buried the brave men and women who, in bringing the Christian faith to this country, gave " the last full measure of their devotion ". They knew that they faced the certainty of loneliness and the imminent risk of death. Yellow fever decimated them and their families. But still they came. They belong to the martyrs of Christianity as surely as those who faced persecution for their faith. The fortitude which they showed is the sure foundation upon which your work has been based. Ghana salutes these men and women who gave their lives for the enlightenment and welfare of this land.

To-day the risks, thank heaven, are less, but the need for devoted service such as they gave is as great as ever. As Ghana develops its economy and diversifies its way of life, new challenges of a vital and testing type lie before us. The hold of tribalism is slackening. The old social disciplines based upon tribal religion and fetishism are growing weaker. Young people are coming into the towns, drawn by new opportunities of living and working. But they are not always ready for the attendant risks of their emancipation. Here is a field in which priest, pastor, educator and social worker must all co-operate to ensure that we educate our young people for genuine maturity, not for irresponsibility and cheap pleasure. I believe a conference such as yours can do immeasurable good if you face in a concrete fashion this moral challenge of young emergent Africa and bring to it the vision and the steadfast service shown by those who have walked before you in the missionary field.

There is another reason for welcoming with special emphasis the representatives of thirty-five different countries gathered here to discuss their common problems. This is, unhappily, not a time in which unity and common understanding and mutual good-will are dominant forces in the world. Here in Ghana we are engaged upon the task of building a new nation. The task will be beyond us if all the groups—religious, racial, tribal—that make up Ghana insist on their separateness and underline what divides them and not the truths and purposes that hold them together. All of you here, from different nations, from different religious professions, are nevertheless met together in common concern and charity. You will, I know, understand me when I say that your spirit seems to me to be profoundly in keeping with the teachings of our Lord Jesus Christ. In this season we are celebrating the birth of a Lord and Saviour whose coming was designed to bring " peace to men of good-will ". But how can there be good-will if Christians think more of their differences than of their whole-hearted devotion to the God of all ? Above all, how can the Christian message be spread effectively to the hopeful and inquiring masses of Africa if it does not come to them rooted in charity " which is the bond of perfection " ?

Nor do I think that this fundamental message of peace and good-will is confined to men solely in their religious efforts. The Christmas message was never more needed in the world at large than it is to-day, and I would plead with you when your conference has ended, when you return to your own countries scattered over the face of the earth, that you should take back with you from this place a message and a challenge. You see Africa. You see the ambitions and hopes of millions of Africans who, so far, have had the crumbs of civilization falling from the rich tables of the western world. Africans of to-day are only at the beginning of their adventure. They need education. They need advancement. They need capital without which no progress to the higher opportunities of life is possible. Yet what do we Africans see when we look abroad? We see vast wealthy nations pouring out their treasure on sterile arms. We see powerful peoples engaged in a futile and destructive armaments race. We see the precious capital that might help to raise up Africa and Asia flung away to potential destruction. What has this to do with the Christian charity proclaimed by the west? Or the human brotherhood we hear so much about from the east? Seen from the angle of Africa's needs and hopes, the Great Powers' rivalry looks like one thing only—a senseless, fratricidal struggle to destroy the very substance of humanity.

So I would say that the unity that you represent here and the further unity which you seek in these talks, are symbols of the whole world's profoundest need. We salute your efforts. We are proud that Ghana should be the scene of your deliberations and we pray that the values you stand for and the hopes you represent may prevail in your hearts, in the development of this young country and in the great family of mankind.

29th December, 1957.

IV

SELECTED PAPERS RESULTING FROM
THE ASSEMBLY

THE WORK OF THE COMMITTEES AT GHANA :
A SUMMARY

By

THE EDITOR

THE committees in the Ghana Assembly were concerned
with administrative matters on which directives and
decisions were required for the continuing work of the
I.M.C. The full text of their reports has not therefore
been included in this volume, which is not primarily concerned with the Assembly as an administrative body. For
the full and authoritative texts of their reports reference
should be made to the " Minutes of the Assembly of the
International Missionary Council, Ghana ".

The matters discussed in the committees have, however,
a bearing on the broader issues with which this volume is
concerned. It has therefore seemed advisable to include
the following summary of the points in their reports which
relate to these broader issues. The recommendations
referred to in the summary were approved by the Assembly.

The Committee on the Study Programme of the I.M.C. recommended the carrying forward of the " Studies in the Life
and Growth of the Younger Churches ", through a series
of studies ' in depth ' of the Church in selected situations,
similar to the study already undertaken in Uganda ;

> Each study should be focused upon the quality of ' alive-
> ness ' in the Church as a whole, in the local congregation

and in the individual Christian, which is revealed by their responsiveness toward the call of the living God within the changes and challenges of their total environment ; . . . the objective should be to assess the factors which promote and those which stultify the responsiveness.

The Committee also recommended a study in the field of theology of mission, having as its focus " What does it mean in theological terms and in practice in the ecumenical era for the Church to discharge its mission to the world ? ", the study :

> to include the biblical and theological basis and goal of mission and a theological evaluation of the existing structures expressing the missionary responsibility of the Churches, and of those which are emerging.

It also recommended the approval of the undertaking of a joint study with the Department of Evangelism entitled " The Word of God and the Living Faiths of Men ", concerned with the encounter with non-Christian religions.

The Committee on the Structure of Co-operation in Mission :

> aware of the fact that in many countries constituent Councils of the I.M.C. are not fully representative of all the Christian groups engaged in the evangelistic task . . .

and feeling that the work of the Assembly had been enriched by the participation of observers from such groups :

> urged all Councils to take fresh initiative in seeking to increase the range of their fellowship and to secure the participation of such groups as are now outside its fellowship in the common task, thus fulfilling the primary purpose for which the Councils exist.

It called attention to the statement of the Willingen meeting on this subject.[1]

It drew the attention of Councils to the concern for " mission in unity " expressed at the Willingen Meeting, quoting from the Willingen Statement.[2] It expressed its

[1] Willingen Minutes, p. 58.
[2] Willingen Minutes, pp. 57–58.

concern for countries in which no councils exist and requested Councils in neighbouring countries and officers of the I.M.C. to "take such steps as will foster 'local' initiative in the matter ".

It welcomed the proposals made at Prapat, March 18th–27th, 1957, for the formation of an East Asia Christian Conference, recognizing " its great significance for the ecumenical movement " and expressing " its keen desire to co-operate in working towards the goal of a permanent East Asia Christian Conference ". Action was accordingly taken to enlarge the East Asia Secretariat of the I.M.C. and W.C.C., to define its wider functions, and to accept the Interim Committee appointed by the Prapat Conference as the Committee which will guide it in its appointed task until the first meeting of the East Asia Christian Conference.

It was felt to be too soon to appraise the significance of this regional development in relation to developments of a similar character in other regions in the world.

The Committee on the Ministry, in the course of its discussion of the whole range of problems connected with the ministry, had presented to it a proposal for a gift by Mr. John D. Rockefeller, Jr., through the Sealantic Fund Inc., of $2,000,000 for the setting up of an I.M.C. Theological Education Fund for the advancement of theological education in Asia, Africa and Latin America. This gift was conditional on mission boards undertaking to provide a like amount over the next five years. Nine American boards had pledged themselves to do so. The Assembly welcomed these generous actions, recognizing :

> . . . the great potential importance of this undertaking for the Christian world mission. It is convinced that such a project should be international in support and operation, and therefore urges every member body of the I.M.C. to make additional contributions to the Fund.

The Assembly set up a Theological Education Fund Committee to administer the Fund, laying down the main principles to guide its operations, and also a Standing Committee on the Ministry (with overlapping membership) for the implementation of the recommendations of the surveys of theological education already carried out by the I.M.C., the completion or renewal of the task of survey, the holding of consultations and interchange of personnel, including special attention to the development of " indigenous theology ", etc.

The Committee on New Forms of Mission noted that :

> . . . the period since the Willingen Meeting has been characterized by increasing recognition on the part both of younger Churches and older Churches that nothing less than the whole of the emerging world Christian community must become the base of the mission of the Christian Church. This vision has already begun to be matched by action and is the truly new factor in the present situation.

But the Committee also noted that " despite Willingen's clear statement of its new insights and concerns, few new forms of mission have as yet arisen from that stimulus ". After reviewing certain developments in different parts of the world, it observed that " little has yet been achieved in implementing Willingen's vision of recruiting laymen as non-professional missionaries ", which " continues to be a subject of great concern and potentiality ", and it continued :

> Neither has the call for more simple, largely voluntary and less institutionalized forms for discharging the Church's functional tasks resulted so far in any outstanding new experiments ; it has, however, put institutional work in its proper perspective in relation to the central evangelistic task. . . . A survey of the past five years seems to indicate that the clues to many effective new forms and methods of mission are to be found in the Willingen concerns and recommendations, together with further insights already gained. . . . We feel impelled not so much to seek new forms, but to urge further experimenting with and far more widespread use of the relatively new forms which are already in view.

The Committee's recommendations commended to Churches and Councils exchange of personnel (for which it recommended guiding principles), the use of Christian laymen as non-professional missionaries (" multi-directional and not simply from older Church to younger Church areas "), the new institutes for the study of non-Christian religions, and Christian literature (" the actual use of this tremendous instrument remains wholly inadequate ") as forms of mission which should be developed.

The Committee on Missions and Inter-Church Aid considered the collaboration between the I.M.C. and the Division of Inter-Church Aid and Service to Refugees of the World Council of Churches, reviewing the various administrative arrangements since the agreement in 1953 setting forth the plan of co-operation between the I.M.C. and the W.C.C. in these matters. On its recommendation the Assembly approved " recommendations of the Joint Committee in the matter of policies and procedures in the collaboration of the I.M.C. and the Division of Inter-Church Aid, and requested the Joint Committee to continue to study them ". It reviewed a plan of co-operation between the I.M.C. and the Division in relation to " non-emergency projects ", which on its recommendation the Assembly approved and referred to the Joint Committee. The Committee dealt also with certain other detailed matters referred to it, and commended the subject of its working paper, " The Mission and Service Programme of the Church ", to continued study by the I.M.C., recognizing that :

> Service and mission are related aspects of the life and work of the Church and that specialization or administrative arrangements must not separate them to the point of seeming to throw them into opposition with one another.

March, 1958.

PROPOSED INTEGRATION OF THE WORLD COUNCIL OF CHURCHES AND THE INTERNATIONAL MISSIONARY COUNCIL

(a) SUMMARY OF THE DISCUSSION IN PLENARY SESSIONS ON THE PROPOSED INTEGRATION OF THE I.M.C. AND THE W.C.C.

By

THE EDITOR

[*Note :* The following paragraphs endeavour to summarize the main points made in the discussion of this
subject in the first three plenary sessions devoted to it (viz.,
January 2nd at 4.30 p.m. and January 3rd at 10.0 a.m. and
4.30 p.m.). It does not attempt to summarize the discussion
at two subsequent sessions (January 6th at 8.30 p.m. and
January 7th at 4.30 p.m.), which were occupied chiefly with
consideration of the draft resolutions submitted by the Steering Committee on the basis of the earlier discussions, since
the outcome of these later sessions is to be found in the
Preamble and Resolutions of the Assembly (p. 165). Some
points of a general character made during these later sessions
have, however, been included in this summary.]

THE discussion of the proposals for the integration of the
I.M.C. and the W.C.C. moved within two main areas :
(1) The reasons of a general kind for and against the
integration of the two world bodies. (2) The effect of such
integration ' locally ', i.e., within national and regional
areas. In addition (3) some comments and suggestions
were made on specific points in the " Draft Plan of Integration " prepared by the Joint Committee (page references
to this plan refer to the pamphlet *Why Integration ?* [1] which
was distributed to all members of the Assembly, and in
which the Plan is printed in full).

[1] By E. A. Payne and D. G. Moses, Edinburgh House Press, 1957.

156

1. REASONS FOR AND AGAINST THE INTEGRATION OF THE TWO
   WORLD BODIES

The arguments advanced in favour and against integration may be roughly grouped under five heads, though
there can be no hard-and-fast divisions between them.

(1) Integration is the appropriate outcome of the trends
of development which have brought the two bodies to their
present situations. This trend of historic development was
referred to by many speakers, both those who favoured and
those who were opposed to integration. Reference was
made to : (a) The fact that it was the missionary movement
which gave rise to the movement towards unity (both inter-
nationally and in the lands of the ' younger ' Churches).
This point was especially emphasized by several speakers
from Councils in Asia. (b) The development of the
' association ' of the two bodies, especially in their joint
activities, the Churches' Commission on International
Affairs, the East Asia Secretariat, the Division of Studies,
the ' emergency ' activities of the Division of Inter-Church
Aid, and the Joint Committee. (c) The concern of both
bodies with ' mission and unity '. (d) The increase in
common planning in response to specific needs. (e) The
geographical and functional overlapping, as more Churches
in Asia and Africa become members of the W.C.C., and
as the integration of Church and mission takes place
locally, especially in Asia, and in world confessional bodies.

This historical trend was diversely interpreted. For some,
it was " the inherent logic of events ". Others saw in it
the result of " the pressure of the Holy Spirit ". The latter
interpretation was questioned by several (both those favour-
ing and those opposing the plan) on the ground that the
integration of the two world bodies was a purely organizational question. For two speakers, the trend implied that
" things had gone too far " for the plan to be opposed even
by those who regarded it as a mistake.

(2) Integration was commended for theological reasons,

such as : that mission and unity belong together ; mission is of the *esse* of the Church ; the Church needs mission and missions need the Church ; " theological consistency" requires that the two world bodies should become one. Reference was made to the summary of these theological considerations in the introduction to the Plan, p. 29, viz. :

> A basic and long-forgotten truth is being re-discovered in our time, which might be stated thus : the *unity* of the Church and the *mission* of the Church both belong, in equal degree, to the *essence* of the Church. If Christian churches would be in very truth the Church, they must carry the Gospel into all the world. They must also strive to achieve the unity of all those throughout the world for whom Jesus Christ is Lord. This truth has already become manifest in the life of both the world bodies. It has led them into association with each other and now obliges them to go further. They exist to help the churches to witness to the wholeness of the Gospel and must, therefore, seek to express the wholeness in their own life.

The theological arguments were challenged on the grounds that (1) the question is an organizational one, and the real issue is obscured by being taken into the sphere of theology ; (2) " that mission and unity belong together " says something about church and mission relationships, but not about the relationships of the W.C.C. (which is not a church), and the I.M.C. (which is not a mission) ; it does not necessarily involve the administrative unity of the two organizations. (3) Church history and the contemporary scene provide evidence that mission can be fulfilled without unity ; the most active groups in mission to-day (amongst whom are some whose work is undoubtedly effective) are Pentecostalists and other ' evangelicals ' and the Roman Catholics ; yet they are not notable for their concern for unity. (4) It was a tenable theological position that only in mission shall we begin to understand what is the unity which God wants for His Church ; this view questions the presuppositions about organic unity in the current ecumenical discussion.

(3) Integration was commended on the ground that it would put mission at the heart of the ecumenical movement. (References were made to the introduction to the Plan, p. 31 and pp. 36–38). It would mean that the Churches could not meet together without being faced with their responsibility for mission. Several speakers referred to the importance of the 'younger' Churches as they became members of the W.C.C., finding mission at its centre. Some considered that integration would facilitate the development by the 'younger' Churches of their missionary outreach ; one speaker gave this as the reason for his council's approval of integration for which otherwise it felt no enthusiasm. On the other hand, reference was made to the fear of some lest ' evangelical zeal ' should be sacrificed for the sake of a ' nominal unity '.

(4) Integration was held to be necessary by those who considered that there was no justification for the continued existence of two separate world bodies. They pointed out that Churches, both ' older ' and ' younger ', especially those in which the mission was an integral part of the church organization, were perplexed by having to deal with two separate world bodies. The continued separation of what belongs together leads to tension and embarrassment in the work of the two bodies themselves, which, it was suggested, would increase the longer the separation continued. Several speakers considered that the bringing of the two bodies together would strengthen the response of Christians to the challenge of non-Christians and of the changes in the social and political scene. Several speakers who had been associated with both the W.C.C. and I.M.C. spoke of the similarity in the outlook and purposes of the two bodies.

On the other hand, there were those who questioned whether the integration of the two world bodies would in fact reflect the reality of the local relationships of church and mission in the world generally. Two speakers contended that the cause of mission and the cause of unity could best be served by a continuance of the present relationship of ' association ', several others expressed their doubts of this view. One speaker referred to fear that many had that integration would result in the creation of a ' mammoth organization '.

(5) The ' Draft Plan ' was commended because it would conserve in the new body all that was represented by the I.M.C. Assembly, which was virtually unchanged in the proposed integrated body (see p. 34), and is provided with an interim body to implement its decisions (the Division, see p. 35). But one speaker thought the plan implied absorption rather than integration.

2. THE EFFECT OF INTEGRATION, NATIONALLY AND REGIONALLY

A considerable number of speakers expressed concern about (a) the possible divisive effect on national Councils (both member Councils of the I.M.C. and non-members) of a decision to integrate ; (b) the probability that some groups who were feeling their way into co-operative organizations would as a result turn away from them ; (c) the probability that some Councils would withdraw from the I.M.C. if it moved towards integration. These risks were widely recognized, both by those who favoured and those who were opposed to the proposals, but diverse views were expressed as to the conclusions to be drawn from them regarding a decision on the proposals. Amongst the points made in this connection were the following :

(1) The very great importance of local co-operation was stressed by many. The representative of one Council said that if such local co-operation could only be maintained, following a decision to integrate, by withdrawal from the international body, then such withdrawal must take place. On the other hand, representatives of other Councils,

which were equally concerned to maintain local co-operation, and which also included member bodies who would
not feel able to be linked with an integrated international
body, considered that an arrangement could be devised in
the constitution of a national council whereby it maintained
its structure and membership but such of its members as
so wished became linked with the integrated international
body.

(2) It was urged by some that integration at the international level should spring from and express national and
regional integration, including the effective local organizational expression of both mission and co-operation. Otherwise integration at the international level might be merely
an escape from real participation in mission and in
co-operation by local bodies.

(3) Some regarded the risk of division locally and of
delaying local negotiations for more inclusive co-operation
as a reason for not proceeding at present with the proposals.
A larger number held that to delay a decision would not
change local situations, but would more probably lead to a
hardening of attitudes. The extent to which a decision to
integrate would disrupt local efforts to extend the range of
co-operation was questioned. Some considered that integration at the international level need not affect local
councils. Some questioned whether, if a decision were post-
poned, the I.M.C. could continue in its present form ; a new
structure was needed for the new circumstances of to-day.

(4) Particular concern was expressed by several speakers
about the need for an instrument of co-operation in tropical
Africa, where the membership of many councils had prevented their joining the I.M.C. because of its ' association '
with the W.C.C. Different conclusions were drawn :
(a) that it was ' too late ' for the I.M.C. to do anything
about promoting co-operation in the region ; (b) that an
" African Christian Council " might emerge, not related to
either the I.M.C. or the W.C.C. ; (c) that there was a
special responsibility on the I.M.C., in the period between

T.G.A.—11

now and a final decision on integration, to foster co-operation in the region and to interpret the plan of integration
and the nature and purpose of the two world bodies.

While there were different views on the above points,
there was general agreement on the need for a period of
education and interpretation ; this need was stressed by a
large number of speakers from many different countries.
It was widely felt that many of the fears about integration
arose from ignorance of or misunderstandings about the
W.C.C. ; reference was made to such points as : (a) that
it was becoming a " super church " ; (b) that its doctrinal
basis was inadequate ; (c) that it lacked evangelical
concern. It was urged that special efforts should be made
to remove these misunderstandsings so that, if there were
withdrawals from national councils or the international
body as a result of integration, they would be based on
conviction in regard to the actual facts and not on misunderstanding or misinformation. The representative of
the Near East Christian Council stressed the need for time,
also for discussion, especially between representatives of
the Eastern Churches and of the missionary movement, of
the issues involved in Christian witness and proselytism.

3. COMMENTS AND SUGGESTIONS REGARDING SPECIFIC
   POINTS IN THE " DRAFT PLAN OF INTEGRATION "

(a) *Timing of procedure.* Several speakers referred to the
need to allow ample time for consideration of the draft
plan and for the submission of amendments by member
Councils.

(b) *A third form of relationship to the integrated body.* A
request was made on behalf of one Member Organization,
and supported by others in the discussion, that there should
be three types of relationship to the integrated body available to national councils : (i) ' association ' with the
W.C.C. and ' affiliation ' to the Commission on World
Mission ; (ii) ' affiliation ' to the Commission only, and
(additional to the present proposals) ; (iii) a ' fraternal '

or 'consultative' relationship with the Commission. It was pointed out that a similar arrangement obtained in the National Council of the Churches of Christ in the United States of America.

(c) *A new world body.* It was urged that stress should be laid on the fact that the integrated body would be a new organization and not simply the continuance of either of the present bodies. This, it was urged, should result in the Central Committee of the new body being a reconstituted committee, and in the provision for the representation of the Commission on World Mission and Evangelism on the Nominations Committee of the new body. One speaker suggested that a new name should be found for the new body.

NOTES

1. During the discussion, Metropolitan James of Melita (present at the Assembly as a consultant) read a statement on the Orthodox view of the proposed integration, the last paragraph of which is as follows :

> To summarize what I have so far said : the question of integration is envisaged by the Ecumenical Patriarchate as a rather technical or organizational question, and as such it is given all necessary attention. I like in any case to stress and repeat that the Ecumenical Patriarchate is guided in the discussions and study of the subject by its concern for the W.C.C. It would never vote for any radical amendment of the W.C.C. Constitution nor would it be prepared to accept any change in the W.C.C. 'ecclesiology' as declared in the well-known Toronto document. Finally, the Ecumenical Patriarchate will insist on the two principles (a) that the sole aim of 'missions' should be to reach peoples yet unconverted to Christ and never to proselytize among the members of other Christian churches, and (b) that the 'missions' should be 'church missions' and should work for the up-building of the Church.

2. In the record of the discussion of the draft resolutions submitted by the Steering Committee, two trends are

apparent : (i) a desire to make a positive statement regarding integration as such ; (ii) a desire not to override the views of the minority in the Assembly, and those whom they represented, and to leave the fullest opportunity for further consideration of the plan. The outcome of both trends is seen in the Assembly's Preamble and Resolutions on Integration, considered as a whole (p. 165 ff.).

February, 1958

(b) RESOLUTIONS OF THE ASSEMBLY

THE Assembly of the International Missionary Council meeting in Ghana (in plenary sessions and in committees) discussed the proposal to integrate the World Council of Churches and the International Missionary Council. The resolutions appended below for transmission to the Member Organizations are an attempt to interpret the mind of the Assembly.

A considerable majority of the Assembly accepts integration in principle. There is strong support for integration from Councils of Asia and North America and from at least one Council in Latin America, while there is a favourable attitude towards it in such areas as Australia and in several of the European Councils. Serious reservations are held, mainly in parts of Africa and Latin America, and by certain Councils in Northern Europe and by individual delegates.

The Assembly has had before it a Draft Plan of Integration prepared by the Joint Committee of the World Council of Churches and the International Missionary Council. Some member Councils, having studied this Plan, have reported favourably upon it. Others have reported serious questions and reservations. Some Councils have not yet studied the Plan itself.

The missionary movement has resulted in a new world Christian community ; this has within itself the possibility of becoming a world-wide missionary community.

This can be achieved particularly because the two world organizations operating in this field belong together. They have been growing together. But serious questions, misunderstandings and fears abound. Time must be given for a thorough study of the issues by all concerned. The

Assembly would refer its member Councils to the record of the debate in the Minutes of the Ghana Assembly for the full statements of those who favour and oppose integration.

The Assembly is convinced that the Christian fellowship in mission must be conserved. To this end we must make the widest possible provision for those who with us would make Jesus Christ known, loved and obeyed, but who cannot go with us the whole way organizationally.

The Assembly believes that in times such as these it must move forward. The Assembly is also convinced that in every possible way it must seek to reconcile the views and convictions of all concerned in order that we may advance together in putting the world mission of the Church at the heart of the Christian community.

In full recognition of the above considerations the Assembly approves the following resolutions :

RESOLUTIONS

Resolved that :

1. The Ghana Assembly of the International Missionary Council, having reviewed the steady growth of the relationship of association between the I.M.C. and the W.C.C. and having considered with care the opinions of delegates, and those of the Christian Councils whose views have been presented, accepts in principle the integration of the two Councils, and desires further steps to be taken towards this goal.

2. The Assembly is of the opinion that such integration requires not only an instrument to define and establish the nature of the new organization, which, as the Assembly believes, will result, but also a much wider growth of understanding, mutual confidence and co-operation at local levels.

3. The draft Plan of Integration, prepared by the Joint Committee of both organizations, is a generally suitable instrument for integration. The Assembly accordingly commends it to member organizations. It

welcomes the opportunity for further study, comment and criticism for amendment and further improvement of the Plan. The Assembly believes that the purposes of mission, promoted and furthered across the years by the I.M.C., are safeguarded and can be advanced through the proposed Commission on, and the Division of, World Mission and Evangelism.

4. The Assembly recognizes at the same time the sincere and deep concern of some of those, now closely associated with Member Organizations, and others who, although not so associated, have contributed notably to the advancement of world mission and evangelism, lest integration should mean the loss of missionary vision and thrust, and a relinquishment of the purposes for which the I.M.C. was founded.

5. The Assembly believes that the criticism of integration which has arisen from this concern, derives in part from a misunderstanding of the W.C.C. and ignorance of the already existing relations between the two organizations. Accordingly, and also for the reasons given in Resolution 2, the Assembly directs the I.M.C. Secretariat to give special attention to the instruction of its own constituency and of all Christians, by literature or other means and by visits of I.M.C. Secretaries, particularly in Africa and Latin America.

6. Since there is much evidence that time is needed to allow further unhurried consideration, the Assembly invited the W.C.C. to consider if it can by any means defer its proposed World Assembly of 1960 to 1961.

7. Meanwhile, the Ghana Assembly directs the Finance Committee to endeavour to provide in the quadrennium budget an increased allocation for secretarial travel, so that the purposes cited in Resolution 5 may be actively pursued. Such travel should also aim at enabling the I.M.C. to serve the needs of all who are devoted to world mission.

8. In commending the draft Plan to member organizations for further study, the Assembly draws their attention to suggestions which have been voiced in the Assembly itself, and which, at the same time, it transmits to the attention of the Joint Committee. Among these suggestions are the following :

(a) The draft Plan provides for affiliation of member Councils to the Commission on World Mission and Evangelism. It should also provide for other links with the Commission by some other form of mutually satisfactory relationship.

(b) The preamble to the draft Plan recognizes that " Churches and Councils in different regions are in different stages of development and have differing perspectives in regard to the ecumenical ideal ". The Plan further states that " the needs and developments within the regions themselves must determine the pattern of the ecumenical service given and received ". The Assembly asks the Joint Committee to give further attention to this aspect and to study ways in which regional variations could find a place in the Plan.

(c) A re-examination should be made of the manner of the composition of the Central Committee to assure adequate representation of the Commission on World Mission and Evangelism.

(d) The Commission on World Mission and Evangelism should be adequately represented in the Nominations Committee.

[*Note :* It will be appreciated that at the Assembly and in its committees, suggestions for amendment in detail were made, which are not listed in these Resolutions, but which, under them, will be considered in due course.]

9. In pursuit of the objectives of the above Resolutions, the Assembly give general approval to the following process for I.M.C. action, with power to the Administrative Committee to make the necessary adjustments :

(a) The draft Plan to be again communicated, as soon as possible, to Member Organizations, with the following documents : a report on the relevant discussions of the Ghana Assembly, a copy of these Resolutions, full information on the present divisional organization of the W.C.C. and a request in terms of Resolution 3 above, for further comment and criticism.

(b) Comment from Member Organizations to be in the hands of the I.M.C. Secretariat by April 30th, 1959, and communicated by it to the Secretary of the Joint Committee and to the Administrative Committee.

(c) The final plan, as prepared by the Joint Committee, to be sent early in 1960 to member organizations, this Plan to take the form of a draft Constitution of the new unified body, with a full explanatory memorandum.

(d) The Administrative Committee or an Assembly of the I.M.C. to consider the Plan (Constitution) in 1960 or possibly in the early part of 1961 and, if approved,

(e) to send it to member Councils following the provisions of Cap. XII (2) of the I.M.C. Constitution.

(f) On the expiry of six months the official action of the I.M.C. is to be signified to the Joint Committee and to the W.C.C.

[*Note* : (i) Professional advice should be sought by the I.M.C. at an early stage on the legality of these procedures, and on such matters as the handling of properties and trust funds.

(ii) The above procedure is based on the assumption that the W.C.C. Assembly will be deferred until 1961.]

10. Since it can only be determined in the light of further comment from Member Organizations, whether

another Assembly will be required, this Assembly agrees that the Administrative Committee be given power to decide whether to call such an Assembly which would then assume the powers otherwise allocated to the Administrative Committee in Resolution 9 (d) above.

REPORT ON GROUP DISCUSSIONS

By

THE REV. GWENYTH HUBBLE

Presented to the Plenary Session in the Assembly

IN his report to this Assembly our General Secretary referred to a new phenomenon in East Asia in the ecumenical movement the real significance of which " lies in the fact that it promises to give wider and more practical expression to the truth that the mission of the Church must be the task of the whole Church ". The challenge, he said,

> is to new ventures in partnership which will involve radical changes in traditional methods and attitudes. The opportunity is to be sharers in what, please God, may prove to be a movement of the Spirit by which the whole concept of mission will find a new birth and make a more compelling claim upon the Church in *every* land.

It was the exploration of those new ventures in partnership, involving the radical changes in traditional methods and attitudes, which were wrestled with in the group which had the subject, " What does partnership in obedience mean ? " But some of the other groups also found themselves confronted with that question. It was clear that the phrase from Whitby, 1947, is not liked by some. Objection is, it seems, based on a kind of commercial view of partnership, of older and younger partners, one who puts in the capital and one who does the work, and especially the thought that the partnership can be entered into and dissolved by the decision of the two partners which, it is urged, is impossible for those who are in partnership because Christ has placed them there, partners in obedience to His great command. But the thought behind the phrase is more fundamentally Christian than commercial ; and if given its biblical content can be acceptable to all, though it is generally agreed that our understanding of it and its implications for us are different from those of Whitby, 1947, because all that has happened in the last ten years happened in the growth of the newly independent nations, in the new life in the old religions and in all that led up to and found expression in the Prapat conference. The latter can perhaps best be summarized as the recognition that Church and Mission belong together. The Church, because it is Christ's, is one Church and from Him has received one mission to go into all the world to preach His Gospel, to fulfil with Him His mission to the world.

That may sound obvious as I say it. Yet the groups have seen that it is *not* a basic principle in much of our thinking and speaking or in our practice. One report states, " The Church called to Mission is a community of sinners whose sins have been forgiven." Here I interrupt the quotation to point out, as that same report does, that that forgiveness is of our past sins as churches, in the west and in Africa and Asia, so there is for us all the possibility of a new beginning. I continue the quotation : " The recognition of our common forgiveness is the basis of our partnership in obedience. Within this relationship each branch of the Church is sending and receiving." That is, one part of the Church sending in obedience to Christ for the sake of another part, and at the same time receiving from Christ in and through other parts of His Church. There was clearly in the groups a desire that we determine here at this Assembly to accept this fact of the one Church sent to the world in obedience to Christ, and prove our acceptance in our thinking and speech by refusing to use the terms " sending and receiving countries ", " older and younger Churches ", and to school ourselves to accept the thought of the one mission of Christ's Church. Let the Ghana Assembly mark the end of the usage of those terns which make distinctions between the Churches. We all live and work together in obedience to Christ in partnership, and that means supplementing each other, not duplicating each other's work, not necessarily carrying the same load of responsibility in all areas. One group asked whether partnership had to have a quantitative basis. Obviously not, if it be partnership in obedience to Christ, for He must decide the area and weight of responsibility of each. It was in the effort to think about that in practical terms that the groups faced some big problems and implications. For example, how are decisions to be made about the sending and receiving of missionaries? It was agreed that the Church everywhere has the right to be obedient to Christ, to share responsibility for His universal mission and that mission always has a geographical dimension. But what if the Church to which the missionary is to be sent (be it a Church in Africa or Asia or the west) does not want that missionary, does not judge that it needs him, considers that its mission may be hindered by his coming? Who decides? Obviously the Church of the missionary cannot override the will of the other and force the missionary upon it against its will, but the Church at the other end must accept the right of the Church of the missionary to be obedient to Christ's command. As D. T. Niles has said somewhere, we cannot decide for each other what our obedience means, but we must decide together ; and the groups recognized that that has very great practical difficulties. It was seen, too, that other factors may be decisive as, for example, the refusal of a visa. The preparatory paper on this subject contained some study of 2 Corinthians i-ix, in relation to this problem of partnership in obedience. I quote from the passage making use of chapter i, 17 where there is the phrase " Yes Yes and No No ". " What now is our situation? Would it be too much to say that we have outlived a period in which the older Church was expected to say ' No ', and the younger Church, ' Yes ', and are in a period in which the older

Church says, ' Yes ', and the younger Church says, ' No ' ?
But have we reached that stage of maturity where ' Yes '
and ' No ' may be used freely by both parties, so that true
Christian conversation and true Christian community may
be realized, because all have heard the ' Yes ' of God through
Jesus Christ ? . . . Can the younger Church accept the
older Church, with all its pride, its shortcomings, its heritage,
its guilt by association ?   Can the older Church accept the
younger Church in spite of its smallness, its weakness, its
spirit of independence ?   By ' accept ' conformity is not
implied, but mutual respect for selfhood." One group
made a practical proposal for working out this partnership.
It proposes " an ecumenical operational body " to the
budget of which the Churches would contribute a proportion of their missionary budget, which ecumenical fund
would be administered ecumenically rather than denominationally.   This approach would not be *instead of*, but *in
addition to* the particular missionary programmes of the
Churches.   It would, it was felt, at least mark a first step
in the realization of the world mission of the Church and
constitute a witness to our commitment to this ideal.

So the Church faced its calling to mission to the world,
but one group made itself face the fact of sin inside the
Church and saw that the inner life of the fellowship of the
Church needs to be revived that it may become more
conscious of, and more fit to tackle its evangelistic task.
That group took considerable time in discussing the renewal
of the Church's life and how some parts of the Church
which lack it can be stirred to a sense of mission.   The other
group on that subject talked together of the danger to
mission of extreme nationalism, a nationalism which desires
no foreign aid and says in effect " leave the task of evangelism in our country to us ".   This the group recognized as
opposed to our fundamental faith in the mission of the
whole Church to the whole world and it spoke of the
danger of national Churches.

But the Church in any given country is in the main composed of citizens of that country who, because of their citizenship, their membership of the society of that country, must seek to be loyal to the life of the nation *and* to the Church. One report speaks of Christians being caught in " a dualism of loyalties " and of, for example, the African convert who has never distinguished between the sacred and the secular, who in the community of the Church lives with people opposed to animism and at the same time in his village is in the midst of animistic practice with the fear of ostracism if he refuses to participate, and so he becomes, the group said, a dual personality, which is highly dangerous. The groups discussed the Church's attitude to indigenous social customs and, while recognizing the danger, feel that there is a great need for expressing the Christian faith in indigenous cultural patterns, and in the very structure of society itself. It was said that often the missionary could here be of more help to the Church than the older Church leaders, for many of them were conditioned by the wholesale opposition to indigenous social customs of the missionaries under whom they were trained in their youth. This was therefore seen to be an important point in relation to the training given in theological colleges. From the reports which I received it did not appear that the groups found that they could formulate criteria for distinguishing between acceptable and non-acceptable social customs, but wished to encourage inquiry and experiment. It was said by an African in one group : " We want to be Africans, not black Europeans ", and an Indonesian said : " We want to show that we also are nationalists and revolutionaries, good Indonesians ". There was, as you would expect, difference of opinion over the advisability of forming a Christian party, and reasons were given on both sides. In countries where the whole concept of ' society ' is new and where newly independent governments are taking over social institutions, what is the place and contribution of the Church ? So often, it was said, it is the Government that ' calls the tune ' for the Church. One of the groups which got into a discussion of some of the problems of South Africa made two useful comments arising out of that discusssion :

(a) It is very easy for us all to become concerned about things in other places and neglect the problems and responsibilities that are on our own doorstep.

(b) It is to be noted that when the Christian Church makes pronouncements against injustice those pronouncements are repeated loud and long by the non-Christian world.

This Church which thus strives to take its place in society and nation has its mission to men and women of other faiths. One group noted that nowadays Christians are more in touch with their non-Christian fellow-countrymen than they used to be, and for many there is, as we have already seen, a tension between their solidarity with their fellow-countrymen and their loyalty to Christ, which results in a new kind of co-existence, which may be dangerous. The same group made the important distinction between the classical faiths and the living faiths of men and women who are to be confronted by the Church, not with a comparison of Christianity and their own faith, but with the Gospel, not with a message but with a Person. Christ, it was said, is Christianity's " unique and unassailable element. We must always preach Him." It was pointed out that in the thinking and experience of most ordinary people, religious systems are not normally opposed to one another in theological categories, but religion provides answers to personal needs in the crises of human life. It was added that such answers are often spontaneously syncretistic. There is considerable evidence that non-Christians are nowadays taking Christian ideas and practices into their religious systems. This is not to be regarded as a help to the Christian mission, for those ideas and practices are transformed in the process and the non-Christian feels that he already has Christian values in his own system and is thus immunized against the proclamation of the Gospel. The groups did not have as long a time as they could have used on the problem of communication, but one group made

the important comment that " communication is not only
what we are saying but also what is heard by the other ".
Another group addressed itself to problems of communication, noting the lack of preparation of Christians to meet
men and women of other faiths, and their use of Christian
terms and concepts which are not understood by non-
Christians.

And what, in this situation as the Church faces her calling
to mission, is the place and function of the missionary, the
missionary whether his country of origin be the west or Asia,
Africa or Latin America, and whether he be financed by
that part of the Church from which he comes, or by another
part ? In no group was there apparently any suggestion
that members felt that foreign missionaries had *no* place or
function in their parts of the Church. There was no plea
for the ' limitation ' of which Prof. Freytag spoke, the
absence of missionaries which ensures that the development
of the Church be not impeded, though there was a clear
feeling that in some places certain categories of missionaries
were not required and would not be welcomed. One group
said that there was a place for the missionary who did not
have too clearly defined a job, but had time for friendship
with his colleagues and ordinary folk in the Church. It was
recognized that to-day power is not in the missionary's
hands, and in the type of missionary who wishes to dominate
that fact may lead to frustration but, it was said, " If
authority is replaced by true fellowship with national
colleagues there need be no frustration ". A number of the
groups seem to have spent time on this frustration of the
missionary, but we need to remember that there are a
number of missionaries even in their first term of service who
are not frustrated or who, if they are, allow God to use that
frustration and bring them through it to greater usefulness
in His Church. It was pointed out that the missionary's
frustration arises in part out of a situation for which we have
prayed. Reasons given for frustration were many. Missionaries in India are questioning whether the Church there

really wants them and whether their presence is for the
good of the Church.   For some it arises from uncertainty
as to the future, due to political causes—how long shall we
be able to stay ?   For others it arises from the fact that their
job is not as clearly defined by the Church under which they
work as it was under the missionary society, for the Church
sometimes does not seem to know how best to use them and
there is often for the missionary what Prof. Freytag called
' lost directness '.   The responsibility for frustration was, in
one group, attributed partly to the mission boards who do
not sufficiently prepare the new missionaries for the ' un-
romantic ' situations and jobs to which they come and who
do not lay upon them the obligation to understand the
culture, the religion, the language and thought concepts of
the people.   All that seems to add up to the fact that some
mission boards must still be giving insufficient preliminary
training to their candidates, and perhaps for all of us it
underlines the Willingen insistence that the training period
must include not only preliminary training but also the first
term overseas and the first furlough.   May I remind you of
one sentence in Prof. Freytag's address : " If we would take
seriously our own insight that the younger Churches cannot
answer the word of God in foreign forms of thinking and
expression, we should cease to send missionaries and teachers
and theologians almost untrained for understanding the
spiritual tradition of the special area in which they serve."
Another reason for frustration, it was suggested, was the
economic factor—housing, stipends, cars, etc.   And one
group seriously urged that there be honest reconsideration
of the problem of the differences in standards of living not
only as between the missionary and his national colleague,
but also as between American missionaries and others.

All this discussion seems to have lessons for the missionary,
the mission boards and the Church to which the missionary
goes.   To the missionary it says that he will be welcomed if
he does not wish to dominate, if he is able to be truly
Christian in his relationship even if he is not given so much

opportunity for activism as his predecessors. He must be ready as far as it is wise and possible to become one with the Church to which he goes and ready for a period of frustration which, if offered to Him, God will use. To the mission boards it says : choose people who can fit into this kind of situation and be ready to find the people with special qualifications when they are asked for, and then prepare and train them for the situation to which they go and for being the kind of people they need to be. Of Churches who receive missionaries it asks that they be ready to undertake the continued training of the new missionary, teaching him well the language and the thought forms, initiating him into the life of the people to whom he has come, helping him to understand their culture and seeking with him to find where and how he can best serve the Church. Both groups appealed to those Churches who receive new missionaries to have a real sense of pastoral responsibility towards them and to give them true nurture in the life of Christ's people.

These lessons if well learned should enable missionaries of all countries to have a place and a function in the mission of the Church at this hour and make it possible for them, exercising all the gifts with which God in His wisdom has endowed them, to serve His Church and mission in the countries to which they go.

THE CHRISTIAN MISSION AT THIS HOUR

Statement received by the Assembly and commended to the Member Organizations of the I.M.C.

[The following statement seeks to share with those in whose name the Assembly of the I.M.C. met at Ghana some thoughts on the central subject which underlay its discussions, " The Christian Mission at this Hour ". It is not a statement formally adopted by the Assembly, but an interpretation of certain aspects of its thought, and particularly of certain convictions which came home to those who shared in it with fresh insistence or in a new form.]

I

THE Christian world mission is Christ's, not ours. Prior to all our efforts and activities, prior to all our gifts of service and devotion, God sent His Son into the world. And He came in the form of a servant—a servant who suffered even to the death of the Cross.

This conviction was emphasized by the Chairman in his opening address. We have seen it to be the only true motive of Christian mission and the only standard by which the spirit, method and modes of Christian missionary organization must be judged. We believe it is urgent that this word of judgment and mercy should be given full freedom to cleanse and redeem our present activities, lest our human pride in our activities hinder the free course of God's mission in the world.

II

But we are none the less fellow-workers with Christ in His mission. That is ground for humility, not for pride. For He trusts *us* with *His* mission. " All power is given to *Me* in heaven and on earth. Go *ye* therefore and make disciples of all nations, baptizing them into the name of the Father and of the Son and of the Holy Spirit "—not into your own name, nor the name of your Church or culture. Christ trusts us to discharge His mission in His form, the form of a servant, a servant whose characteristics are humility and suffering.

III

So we are responsible. Each of us in his own place, each local company of Christ's people, each church in its organized life cannot be Christ's without being His missionary servant. A vague and generalized acceptance of the world mission is no substitute for responsible action in the discharge of missionary obedience.

But we are responsible to one another in Christ. We are called in Him to recognize with gladness that our fellow-Christians, our neighbouring congregations, our sister denominations in our own and other lands are called by the same missionary Lord, and need the same freedom as we ourselves do to respond to His calling.

There is a tension which can easily become a contradiction—the tension between missionary passion and a due regard for the claims of the Christian fellowship. It has shown itself at many points in our discussions, as we have talked together about the place and function of the missionary, the structure and tasks of the Christian Councils, and especially in our discussion of the proposal that the I.M.C. and the W.C.C. should become one body. We have not seen how the contradiction can be removed. It may well be that the tension is one that is inherent in the Christian life. We have, however, we believe, discerned some points at which the tension can be creative within the fellowship.

IV

The essential precondition is that we all remember constantly that the mission is Christ's, not ours. For that reason it transcends our organizations. They all stand alike under His judgment and mercy, and none can claim finality or perfection.

We have been given some glimpses of what this means. Our discussions have repeatedly shown us that the distinction between ' older ' and ' younger ' Churches, whatever may have been its usefulness in earlier years, is no longer valid or helpful. It obscures the status of Churches before God, and so obscures the truth that precisely in the fact of being churches they are all equally called to obedience to their one missionary Lord. Churches differ in resources and in opportunity for mission ; but those differences are not in principal differences between ' older ' and ' younger ' Churches. Within their fellowship in Christ, Churches give and receive from one another in their missionary task ; but such giving and receiving no longer takes place solely between ' older ' and ' younger ' Churches. If they *are* churches, they are all alike called to mission.

But the mission to which they are called is not *their* mission ; it is Christ's mission. The interests of the individual churches and of individual missionary organizations are therein also transcended. To seek first to safeguard the interests, the activities, the sphere of influence of our church, our mission, our confessional body is in the end a denial of mission, a refusal to be a servant. As the General Secretary reminded us in his report, we must ask of any proposal for new work, new developments, new patterns of co-operation, not " How will this affect us ? ", but " What is God's will in this situation ? " Since the mission is not ours but Christ's, any kind of claim to the sole control of any area in the interests of one ecclesiastical body, whether an ' older ' or a ' younger ' Church, seems to us incompatible with a recognition of our common calling in Christ as missionary servants. Equally incompatible with that calling is a determination to preach the Gospel in some particular area in one particular way, without regard to fellow-Christians in the area concerned. We do not commend the Gospel by ignoring the existence of those who

also name the name of Christ. Freedom in obedience to
the mission of the Gospel is freedom to serve the fellowship,
not to deny it.

V

That Christ be proclaimed has been the purpose which
has held us together beneath many divergences. For we
are convinced of the centrality and the urgency of the
continuing missionary task. That urgency has received
many different expressions amongst us. For some, it is
focused in the fact that there are more non-Christians in
the world to-day than when the modern missionary movement began. For others the spectacle of a technological
age which is in danger of deserving the judgment that it
has " exchanged the truth of God for a lie and worshipped
and served the creature rather than the Creator, who is
blessed for ever " arouses the sense of the desperate need
to point men to the already present Lord of all life. Still
others find the renascence of the ancient religions and the
encounter with the Christian faith at a new depth and with
a new directness the point at which the need for Christian
proclamation throughout the world becomes most insistent. But we are all agreed that this is an hour in which
Christians must go out into the world in the name of
Christus Victor.

VI

We do not yet see with full clearness what that going
out must mean in terms of the new forms which the proclaiming of Christ may need to fashion or the new patterns
of relationship it may demand. But two things are clear
to us. First, that we have enough knowledge for present
obedience. There are tasks lying to our hands, new relationships into which we are being called, methods of work
which we know we should reform or abandon. Some of
these immediate tasks are indicated in the actions of the
Assembly. Many of them have been familiar for many

years. In regard to them, it is not knowledge that we lack ; it is the will to do them. That, we believe, is why we still grope for fuller understanding of the nature and form of Christian mission in our day. The condition of receiving further insight is to act upon what we have. Ideas are no substitute for decisions ; the exchange of thought is no substitute for action in common obedience.

We believe that at this Assembly we have taken some small steps in obedience in the matters committed to us. We have tried to respond to the missionary God whose words and acts are one. Therefore we believe we have the right to say to you who sent us here, that the mission is Christ's, not ours. Beyond the complexities of inter-church relationships, beyond the safeguarding of organizations, beyond any mistrust of one another, beyond any pride in numbers and size, in devotion and piety, He is calling us out—out beyond the frontiers of the Churches, out beyond the sphere of inter-church relationships, out beyond the traditional patterns of missionary activities, out into a new exposure to Him, out into a new and more real commitment to one another, out into the world where He is the Hidden King, out towards the day of His open Reign —to which the Christian mission moves.

V

THE RÔLE OF THE I.M.C.

*Some Reflections on the Nature and Task of the I.M.C. in the
Present Situation.*

BY

Erik W. Nielsen

[The purpose of this essay is to contribute to the continued
discussion of some of the issues discussed at the Ghana
Assembly.   In order that its author could have the fullest
freedom of expression for that purpose, he was invited to
write solely in his personal capacity.   His essay therefore
expresses his personal views.]

Introduction

There seem to be only two kinds of weather in Scotland
(with due apology to that noble land).   When one can see
the hills, it is going to rain ; when one cannot see the hills,
it is raining.   Embarking upon this essay has a number of
similarities with planning a journey into such conditions,
and it ought really to begin with a most sincere apology for
ever having accepted the invitation to write it ; it takes a
considerable degree of naïvety (it would be presumptuous
to say courage) to undertake this task at this particular
juncture—and even more so if one happens to be a secretary
in the I.M.C., who is oneself a part of the structure that is
to be discussed and is therefore also to some extent unable
to look at things objectively, and at other points may be
somewhat inhibited about saying things which perhaps
ought to be said.

A word must be said about the status, or rather lack of

status, of this essay. Although it is included in a volume originating in the Ghana Assembly of the I.M.C. and containing material from this meeting, the present essay is strictly a purely personal attempt at looking at the rôle and function of the I.M.C. ; the invitation to write this article was only accepted on this clear condition and the I.M.C. can take no responsibility whatsoever for views or conclusions expressed in the following pages. In other words, in this essay it is only one person trying to reflect on some of the issues which, as far as he can see, are involved in the question of the task of the I.M.C. at this time ; this also means that the whole thing is necessarily coloured by his own background, his particular way of thinking, the very point at which he stands. All this cannot be avoided ; it can only be hoped that the one-sidedness and the limitations will not distort the picture too much. The intention is not to make an academic study, but rather to participate in a discussion in the hope that this may call forth further discussion on an issue which in its implications is of very far-reaching importance.

This discussion is not being started here ; far from it. It has already gone on for several years in one form or another. It was a prominent feature in the years immediately before 1948 when the World Council of Churches was " in process of formation ", and it has been the underlying issue in practically all I.M.C. affairs since the Whitby conference in 1947. It has been reflected in a number of practical arrangements such as the establishment of the Churches' Commission on International Affairs, the various arrangements regarding Inter-Church Aid, the developments in the field of ecumenical study, etc., etc., and during the last two or three years it has received new sharpness and urgency in the negotiations regarding a possible amalgamation of the I.M.C. and the W.C.C.

It is undoubtedly this last question which, at this juncture, provides the immediate setting for a discussion of the rôle of the I.M.C. When in one of the committees at the Ghana

Assembly the suggestion was made that an essay be written on this subject, the context was clearly the deliberations concerning the I.M.C.–W.C.C. relationship ; at the Ghana meeting the discussions tended to think in terms of organizations, of the possibility of a merger between two organizations which in their basic structures could appear to be incommensurate, and of the consequences of such a merger. At this level the question of the rôle of the I.M.C. is seen primarily in relation to the structure of the ecumenical movement as represented by the World Council of Churches. At present the two are " in association with " one another, a relationship which is more than a nice façade. There *is* a very intimate relationship in consultation and joint action. Should this structural relationship be developed further towards full amalgamation of the two organizations (or, as some prefer to put it, should the I.M.C. " join the W.C.C.") ? What are the reasons for and against this ? What place should an I.M.C., or a possible Commission and Division of World Mission, occupy within the World Council ? What would be the functions of such a commission and division and what sort of organizational structure could be developed which would further and not hamper the central purpose of such an amalgamation ? What would be the consequences of such a move, negative and positive ? All these questions are important and are being wrestled with by both organizations through their Joint Committee—and yet the question of the rôle of the I.M.C. goes much further and deeper than that. After all, the organizational relationship to the World Council of Churches is really a secondary question which has its significance, but should not be allowed to overshadow or so to fill the picture that it becomes impossible to see other and more important issues. Organizational amalgamation with the W.C.C. will not in itself solve any of the very real questions with which the world mission of the Church is faced to-day. If approached as an end in itself, it may on the contrary become a means of escaping into organizational clarification and aggrandizement, escaping from painful and patient confrontation with questions which are pursuing us and will go on doing so. This amalgamation will not basically solve anything, but it may provide us with a new frame within which a picture is to be painted. But what picture? Here the question of the rôle of the I.M.C. appears in a different perspective; it goes deeper and becomes more confused and difficult.

At this level the I.M.C. is facing fundamental questions regarding its own nature and task quite apart from the organizational relationship to the W.C.C. (although the way in which this relationship is worked out will have its profound influences upon the context within which the I.M.C. will be able to come to grips with this issue). There are undoubtedly some who would rather see the I.M.C. saying " No ! " to the proposed amalgamation with the W.C.C. and continuing as it is. *But* is this not an illusion? Can the I.M.C. continue as it is? Saying " No ! " to inte-gration with the W.C.C. means saying " Yes ! " to something else—to what? We cannot escape this question ; it is no mere accident that I.M.C. meetings, such as Willingen in 1952 and Ghana in 1958, seemed strangely unable to give anything like a clear or strong lead. This was singularly conspicuous at the Ghana meeting. Although Willingen produced much of considerable value, yet it was difficult for the participant to avoid the impression that somehow the direction was lost, that there were many valuable discussions, but that it was not at all clear in which direction they were leading—and the temptation was often to try to solve real and difficult questions by a bit of impressive phraseology and drafting (this temptation, one presumes, is not exactly limited to the I.M.C.). All this has something to do with the question of the rôle of the I.M.C. ; it is very largely a reflection of the situation not only in its member units, the various missionary and Christian councils, but in particular in the traditional missionary movement. Here the I.M.C. is part and parcel of that transition stage in which this whole

movement stands at the present time. The question of the
rôle of the I.M.C. at this time is indissolubly linked up with
this background and cannot be discussed apart from it. The
questions which the missionary movement has to face are
therefore also in one form or another involved in a discussion of the I.M.C. As was pointed out at the Ghana
Assembly, previously the missionary societies had problems ;
to-day they themselves are problems—the same applies to
the I.M.C.

And at the bottom of all this there is a fundamentally
theological question. There have been much discussion,
many statements and many books written on the question
" Why Mission ? ". To-day this " Why ? " does not go
deep enough nor does it raise the question radically enough ;
to ask this question is only meaningful if there is already a
clear conception of *what* Mission is ; but it is precisely here
that we are in trouble. The question to-day must be " What
is Mission ? ". The various problems with which the
missionary movement is striving are not just organizational
or structural difficulties, which a good organizer could con-
ceivably disentangle if he were given the freedom to do so ;
there is more in it than just that. We (Churches in the east
and the west) will not be able to call to Mission again with a
good conscience and with power, until we have faced clearly
and honestly the fact that we are no longer really sure what
Mission is. We shall, under the power of the Holy Spirit
and in a new listening to the Bible, have to come to grips
with this fundamental question and try to see what this
means for our actual situation, our obligations and tasks.
Only then can we hope to find our " direction " again, to
find new " liberation " in our obedience. Only then can we
hope to be able to break through this strange mixture of
tiredness and frantic, impatient activity which so often seems
to colour our missionary work and discussions and conferences about it. Nor can there be any doubt but that this
question is at the very root of the question regarding the
nature and function of the I.M.C. itself. Here it is true

what was said during one of the discussions at the Ghana
Assembly : " If the trumpet gives an uncertain sound, we
do not put it right by giving it a place in a symphony
orchestra." All this means that the subject of this article
goes far beyond the mere question of the I.M.C. as an
organization, however complicated that question can be in
itself. We shall have to see this in a wider context, although
it cannot be the purpose in a few pages here to give an
analysis of the general missionary situation nor to sketch the
contours of a " theology of Mission ". We shall, however,
have to touch upon all of this, knowing full well that this has
been done much better and more fully in other places.

We shall try to approach our subject in the following
stages. It will first be necessary to glance backwards. The
purpose of this is not to give a brief history of the I.M.C.,
but simply to try, if possible, to see some of the major factors
which have shaped this organization, to try to get a feeling
of its special *ethos* and rhythm, and through it all to get a
firmer perception of what this phenomenon, the International Missionary Council, which we are discussing,
really is and stands for. After that we shall reflect briefly
on some aspects of the Ghana material. Finally we shall
try to gather those lines together and to discuss what this
means for the rôle of the I.M.C. as a part of the ecumenical
movement at this hour.

1. LOOKING BACK—SOME ASPECTS OF THE HISTORY OF THE
   I.M.C.

As early as 1888, in connection with the third International Missionary Conference in London, Gustav Warneck
from Germany presented a plan for the formation of an
international missionary organization, the main structure of
which was virtually the same as that of what later became
the International Missionary Council. Warneck was not
able to be present at the conference and his plan was not
discussed, although it was printed in the report ; the time
was not yet ripe for such ideas. It was, however, an im-

portant indication of what was in the air, and when the
I.M.C. finally became a reality it was not really a new thing,
but basically a consequence of a whole series of developments in the latter half of the nineteenth century, both in
the west and in Asia. The I.M.C. was not started as a
bright new idea ; it came into being gradually and it began
in local situations. It had begun in Germany, England,
America, in China and India years before it came into
existence as an international body.

These beginnings were marked by a whole series of conferences where gradually co-operation, or at least mutual
consultation, began to take form. Already in 1846 a
gathering for German missionary societies met in Berlin,
and in 1866 the first Continental Missions Conference met
in Bremen, and was later to meet every four years. In
Britain a conference (planned by the Evangelical Alliance)
met in London in 1854 and subsequently in Liverpool in
1860, in London in 1879, and again in 1888. In the U.S.A.
a meeting, the Union Missionary Convention, took place in
New York in 1854 ; the best known, however, was the huge
gathering in New York in 1900 which had at its daily
sessions about 4,000 people present. Perhaps even more
important were the gatherings on the fields. They began,
naturally, as local consultations, but soon grew into wider
organizations. In India, the first General Conference of
Bengal Protestant Missionaries met in Calcutta in 1855.
For South India a similar meeting took place at Ootacamund
in 1858. For both areas these marked the beginnings of a
series of most important consultations, and in 1873 the first
all-India conference met in Allahabad. In China, the first
general missionary conference met in Shanghai in 1877.
Similar developments took place in other areas. Such conferences became training grounds for the building up of
methods and techniques of consultation and co-operation
and, more important, they began to mould the outlook of
their participants and to make it natural to discuss one's
own affairs in a wider setting. John Mott could say in 1911

that the Edinburgh conference " has familiarized the
Christians of our day with this idea of looking steadily at
the world as a whole, of confronting the world as a unit by
the Christian Church as a unit ", a somewhat premature
phrase uttered three years before the first World War—
and yet there was a truth in it, a truth which was gradually
being realized, however imperfectly, during these later years
of the nineteenth century.

There were other and most important trends in this
development. We can mention only the various student
movements. Whereas the missionary societies were cautious
and guarded their independence somewhat jealously, these
movements furnished an element of impatience and urgency
which often gave the final stimulus. Further, the student
movements proved to be an excellent training ground for an
astonishing number of first-rate leaders, whom we later find
in the International Missionary Council, and in almost all
the other elements of the ecumenical movement.

It was against this background that the Edinburgh conference met in 1910. This conference is so well known and
so much has been written about it that there is no need to
go into any detail here. As suggested above, Edinburgh did
not mark the beginning of something totally new, nor was
it the end of a development ; and yet, in a sense, it was
both. In his book *Ecumenical Foundations* [1] Dr. Richey Hogg
has aptly described Edinburgh as a lens, " a lens catching
diffused beams of light from a century's attempts at missionary co-operation, focussing them, and projecting them
for the future in a unified, meaningful, and determinative
pattern " (p. 98). The lens caught the beams of light which
were there, and not only the beams in the field of missionary
co-operation but the theological and cultural beams as well.
It focused all this sharply and projected it with power and
conviction, and something new was brought into being.
The lens was set in the strange twilight of the transition from
the nineteenth to the twentieth century. It belonged more

[1] Harper & Bros., New York, 1952.

to the nineteenth than to the twentieth. The cataclysm of
the first World War was looming on the horizon, but at
Edinburgh there hardly seems to have been any premoni-
tion of what was to come and of the extent to which a whole
world was going to be changed in its political geography
and in its whole rhythm of life. The Boxer Rising had
taken place in China and the Japanese had defeated the
Russians in 1905. Nationalism was stirring in various areas.
These things were disturbances, problems to be taken into
account, things to be reckoned with in missionary planning,
but planning as such was still possible. Dr. Hogg says about
Edinburgh, " One is not struck with any display of naïve
optimism at Edinburgh " (p. 138). That is true ; there
was hope, drive, a tremendous feeling of challenge, responsibility and new discovery, something different from naïvety.
And yet there was a basic optimism in the sense that the
world around was still familiar. One only has to read
Dr. Mott's preface (written while still at Edinburgh) to his
book, *The Decisive Hour of Christian Mission*,[1] to sense something of this. Who could see at Edinburgh that the " disturbance " at Port Arthur was a symptom of fundamental
change of the world scene, which was to lead to the kind of
picture for which Bishop Newbigin uses the phrase " the
western part of the European peninsula of Asia " ? [2] Who
could see in its full depth that human progress might also
mean the uncovering of humanity's rebellion against God ?
It belonged to the unfolding twentieth century to bring it
home to us that the tragic is an integral part of history, that
deep irrational forces are at the roots of our being and of
our social structures. The voices of an Adolf Hitler, a Jomo
Kenyatta, a Dietrich Bonhoeffer or a Karl Barth were not
part of the choir at Edinburgh. The lens was placed at the
end of the nineteenth century, but the beams it focused set
in motion—directly or indirectly—in the lives of individual
men and in the thinking of groups and organizations, a

---

[1] Student Volunteer Movement for Foreign Missions, New York, 1910.
[2] *The Household of God*, Lesslie Newbigin. S.C.M. Press, 1953. (p. 11.)

series of impulses which proved to be of decisive importance for the ecumenical movement of the twentieth century.

We are primarily concerned with the International Missionary Council. Edinburgh resolved to set up a Continuation Committee. As the proposal for an International Missionary Committee first seems to have come from Germany (through Warneck in 1888), so also this suggestion came out of Germany, in that the chairman for the German ' Ausschuss ' (the Standing Committee of the German Evangelical Missionary Societies), Dr. Oehler, in 1909 proposed the formation of " an International Committee dealing with international missionary questions ". Virtually the same idea had come up in America, and at one stage Dr. Mott had advocated that Britain, America and Germany together should form an international committee.

While there was and for some time continued to be considerable doubt about the wisdom of setting up a permanent international committee, Edinburgh did set up a Continuation Committee, with the task of carrying forward what had been begun at Edinburgh. It was to avoid " doctrinal or ecclesiastical differences of the various denominations " and would only have an advisory function. One of its tasks was to explore the possibility of forming an international missionary committee. The task was vague, undefined and huge. Two lines of development are of particular interest in our connection.

First, a series of local councils were formed in various parts of the world. During 1912 and 1913 Dr. Mott undertook a series of journeys in Asia, holding conferences with missionaries and nationals and discussing the situation. As a result of that (*and* of previous developments in the areas) a series of national councils came into being. The National Missionary Council in India, the Burma Council of Christian Missions, an Interim Committee in Malaya, the China Continuation Committee, the Continuation Committee in Japan, all came into being as a result of Mott's visits. Out of these developed national missionary councils,

and later when these became councils of churches more
than of missions, national Christian councils. A similar
development took place also in the west. The Conference
of British Missionary Societies with its Standing Committee
was established in 1910 ; after various overtures, the Conference of Foreign Mission Boards in the United States and
Canada in 1907 finally set up a Committee of Reference
and Counsel. In Germany, a Committee of the German
Evangelical Missionary Societies (Ausschuss der deutschen
evangelischen Missionen) had already come into being in
1885. In the Scandinavian countries, missionary councils
were formed in Sweden and Denmark in 1912, and later in
Finland and Norway. It was really a tremendous structure
which was built up within a few years after Edinburgh, and
several more councils were formed in the following years.
They practically all followed the pattern of Edinburgh.
They were consultative bodies only, set up to advise and
help in mutual consultation and common approach to
various specific questions like relationships to governments,
education, etc. They were built on the idea of co-operation
in various practical matters, and a very considerable
number of them included in their constitution in one form
or another the clause from Edinburgh that they would not
interfere in matters concerning " doctrinal and ecclesiastical
differences ". They were in no way subordinate to the
Edinburgh Continuation Committee and did not come into
being primarily because of influence from that Committee,
but because of impulses and forces in their own areas.

The second line of interest in the time of the Continuation
Committee lies in another sphere. At its first meeting, nine
international commissions were set up to deal with matters
like " unoccupied fields ", " missionary preparation ",
" missions and governments ", " Christian education ", etc.
Some of these commissions did useful work, but it was soon
discovered that this was much too cumbersome and unrealistic. If these commissions were really going to justify
their existence, they would have to meet fairly frequently,

which would be a very costly affair, and would constantly pull men out of their own situations where they were most needed. Further, there was a feeling that, at least in some cases, such international committees would only duplicate what really could be better done on a national or regional level. The permanent international commissions were therefore comparatively soon given up and the emphasis put much more upon the national units.

The first World War meant a tremendous test for the new structure. In 1918 the British and American elements formed an Emergency Committee to function in the absence of the Germans on the Continuation Committee. Feelings ran very high in German-Allied relationships. At times it looked as though there was no bridge possible. Yet bridges were built which stood the even harder tests of later years ; but it took time, a long time. Invaluable work was done in order to save German missionary property from confiscation by the Allied powers and to help Continental societies financially.

After the war—with the greatest difficulty—the lines were taken up again. A meeting was called at Crans, Switzerland, in 1920, where careful thought was given to the proposed international missionary organization. With the experiences of the war so fresh in the minds of the participants, such a body was deemed necessary and the conference unanimously agreed to form an " International Missionary Committee " ; it was explicitly stated (with a formulation from a former meeting in 1913) that " the only Bodies entitled to determine missionary policy are the Home Boards, the Missions, and the Churches concerned ". Dr. J. H. Oldham, in the discussions, said that such an organization might mark the start of " something that may represent the beginnings of a world league of churches ". The Crans recommendations were circulated and discussed, and finally, at the meeting at Lake Mohonk, New York, in 1921, the International Missionary Council was formed, to stimulate thinking and investigation on missionary questions, to help co-ordinate activities of missionary organizations, to bring about united action where necessary, to help unite Christian opinion, and to help to bring about justice in international and inter-racial relations—a formidable programme indeed, and one that reflected both the time in which it was conceived and the fact that the new International Missionary Council was the main and central focus of the emerging ecumenical awareness.

We have given considerable space to these beginnings because they throw important light upon the nature of the I.M.C., the background on which it was established and at least some of the factors which gave it its structural form. We have hinted at at least some of the vague lines of a new picture beginning to be drawn towards the end of the last century, of a movement not an organization, a movement with a series of quite different roots, which took different forms in different areas. At one point it became crystallized in the International Missionary Council, and at later stages found other points of crystallization ; but it was the same movement. There were, so to say, different strands in the movement, different trends ; they did not move at the same pace. There were clearly political trends, economic, cultural and theological trends. It is probably true to say that, just as the missionary movement in the nineteenth century was in some considerable way a reflection of the whole cultural and political *ethos* of that time, so this new ecumenical movement of the twentieth century reflected at many points the political, cultural and economic transformations which were taking place after the first World War.

The idea of an international missionary organization was conceived in the nineteenth century, but it came into being in another era, in a time of insecurity and fundamental change. It is difficult to overrate the direct, and perhaps even more the indirect, importance of the I.M.C. during those years between the two world wars.

Dr. Hogg rightly gave his history of the I.M.C. the title *Ecumenical Foundations* ; it proved to be just that—with consequences and implications which very few could have seen in 1910. It is difficult to give a clear picture of the I.M.C. during those years up to the second World War, and in any case there is not space to do so here. It was a strange, many-coloured thing. It was, as someone has said— " demonstrably unworkable " and yet it worked. We do not find a long series of official statements on the basis of which we can discuss the attitude of the I.M.C. to this and that. The I.M.C. was not and has never been inclined to produce statements, and when it has done so they have rarely been of world-shattering importance. The genius of the I.M.C. did not lie in that direction. Nor is it too easy to determine the locus of the I.M.C. It was not primarily to be found in the London or the New York offices, but rather in the national units in America, Britain, China, India and elsewhere in the west and the east. There were quite different questions in these different situations, and from the central offices of the I.M.C. the Secretaries tried to give help, advice and stimulus as far as possible ; but the main responsibility rested with the bodies directly involved and with the local councils. The National Christian Council of India *was* the I.M.C. in India—that was the basic philosophy, however imperfectly it may have worked— with the London or New York offices to be called upon when special help or advice was needed or when questions needed discussion in an international setting. At the centre, in London and New York, there was a staff of two or three senior Secretaries all told—an incredibly small staff which in many respects accomplished the incredible. They were mobile—more so than later with a considerably increased staff—and their influence and that of the I.M.C. as a whole were out of all proportion to the size of the staff.

The activities and concerns of the Council ranged over practically every aspect of missionary work. Attention was given to questions like Christian education with special commissions sent to Africa and India, to Christian literature, Christianity and race, the fight against traffic in narcotics, slavery and forced labour, and several other matters. A special department was set up to study social and industrial questions and their effects upon the Churches in Asia and Africa. At the same time discussion was constantly going on regarding the more specific ' missionary ' questions, the relationship of missions and missionaries to the younger Churches, the training of missionaries, self-support, etc., etc. It is impossible here even to indicate the many and varied matters which were on the Council's agenda at one time or another.

Conferences like Jerusalem in 1928 and Tambaram in 1938 were outstanding events which, with very thorough preparation, discussed some of the most burning issues of the time. In both cases the fundamental debate was not about missionary planning or strategy, but about the essential nature of the Gospel itself. The climate was very different from Edinburgh ; this is particularly noticeable in the case of Tambaram. A profound theological re-orientation had begun to make its impact and to put exceedingly radical questions to our traditional Christian thinking. In Europe a spiritual and cultural battle was developing, forcing Christians to rethink the very fundamentals of the Gospel and to be prepared to take the ultimate stand. There was war in the east, and the familiar pattern of the world was rapidly becoming unrecognizable. With the second World War looming over the horizon, Tambaram went deeper and further than any of the previous I.M.C. conferences, and the most important discussions were about central issues like the Gospel and religion and the nature of the Church.

In the same period other lines were developing. " Faith and Order " and " Life and Work " had come into the picture, and the I.M.C. was no longer the main ecumenical body, although it was still the one which in a special way had a world perspective. In the years immediately prior to the war and during the war, increasing thought and discussion were given to the possibility of forming a World

Council of Churches, in which the three trends would meet. The I.M.C., its Secretaries and its whole perspective of work and interest played a considerable part in these discussions.

The end of the second World War brought in many respects an entirely new picture. In the post-war period the I.M.C. continued as before maintaining contacts with its constituent councils, studying questions like theological training in Africa, and other matters, and being occupied with the numerous questions which find their way into the offices of this organization ; and yet the whole atmosphere was different and a whole number of far-reaching issues claimed attention. The very setting and context for the existence of the I.M.C. was rapidly changing. The World Council of Churches had been established, with its " in association " relationship with the I.M.C., and a number of concerns which had previously taken a prominent place in normal I.M.C. activities were now handled in conjunction with the W.C.C. or more or less completely taken over by the W.C.C.

But there were more important trends in this period after the war. The Whitby meeting of the I.M.C. in 1947 met in an atmosphere of rejoicing after the war and struck a note of confident looking ahead, with its emphasis upon " expectant evangelism " and its talk of " partnership in obedience ", a phrase the contents and implications of which has not yet been fully realized. However, the next two meetings, in Willingen, 1952, and Ghana, 1958, were of a different nature. To some they were just disappointing ; to others they were deeply significant, positively and negatively. At Willingen many important things were said and discussed and yet—to put it somewhat sharply—the meeting could not break through an inner confusion, a being caught up in the internal affairs of missions. A passionate plea at one stage in the discussions for new mobility and new endeavours was eagerly grasped but almost as an escape from ourselves, and it remained standing alongside, unreconciled with all the other aspects of the deliberations where the real problems were. Was all this just a result of insufficient preparation and planning for the meeting ? This, undoubtedly, was one factor, but was there not more in it ? Was it not also a reflection of the general situation of the traditional work of the missionary societies and of the I.M.C. At the Ghana meeting this was even more conspicuous. The question which here occupied the minds of people was the relationship to the W.C.C. and the proposed " integration "—in spite of the efforts on the side of the planners of this meeting to see all this in a wider context. Undoubtedly this had a certain laming effect upon the meeting, but perhaps that phrase from one of the speakers gave expression to the underlying question : " Then missions had problems, but they were not a problem themselves "—a drastic sentence which we should not ignore.

It is a strange line which leads from Edinburgh to Ghana. It is important to remember that this " Edinburgh-line " also goes to Lausanne, 1927, to Oxford, 1937, to Amsterdam, 1948 and Evanston, 1954. Ghana, viz., the I.M.C., is one focal point—and one only—in this whole ecumenical move- ment, which is a movement and not an organization. The call to Mission which was sounded at Edinburgh was also heard in these other meetings. Later we shall discuss some of these things further ; here the brief sketch of the development of the I.M.C. must stop. It will serve as a general background to the following discussions.

Although generalizations are dangerous, and perhaps particularly so in this case, it may be worth while at this stage by way of summing up to indicate a few features which seem to be characteristic of this I.M.C. and which grew up after the first World War. It is clearly realized that these are generalizations which do not apply equally in every situation or even at every time.

First, the I.M.C. is a strongly decentralized structure. It is made up of national or regional councils all over the world (at present there are thirty-eight such councils in membership with the I.M.C.), and it can be said that to a large degree the I.M.C. really has its main life and substance out in these local councils rather than at the centre. This means a tremendous flexibility and variety. Ecumenically speaking, it means that the I.M.C. probably has a wider span than any other ecumenical organization. Not only is there at one end of the keyboard the council which has as close a relationship with the W.C.C. as the W.C.C. constitution will allow, and at the other end the council which is afraid of any relationship with the W.C.C. at all ; but the local membership within one council varies ; in one area the council may have among its members a Christian body which in the neighbouring country cannot or will not become a member of the council in that country ; the council itself is the only authority here ; the I.M.C. has no control or authority of any sort over its members. In this decentralized structure, the " centre " is surprisingly weak. The staff is small, much too small, and it is split up between two central offices, in London and New York. The development of an East Asia Office occurred towards the end of the period and is further evidence of the decentralized structure of the I.M.C.

This flexible structure is, from one point of view, one of the strengths of the I.M.C. The I.M.C. has not built up a strong super-structure, and so it could not carry even the least suggestion of power. It has tried to act realistically, accepting the differences of varied situations and helping those situations in their diversities, rather than imagining that it could act easily towards the world as a whole. It has tried to be more interested in the work in those areas than in promoting itself. All this must be admitted honestly and readily, and yet it also has to be said that in this very conciliar structure is one of the weaknesses of the I.M.C.

It was an accepted principle from the beginning that only the church or missionary society has the right " to determine missionary policy ", but these bodies are structurally only in contact with the I.M.C. through a local council which

itself has no authority over its members ; it is—just like the
I.M.C.—only advisory and consultative. Speaking ideally,
this is precisely as it ought to be. Mutual advice and consultation which, under the power of the Holy Spirit, is frank
and honest can be stronger than the firmest ' control '.   It
means, however, that the I.M.C. is not constitutionally in
direct contact with those bodies which can " determine
missionary policy ". The local council is in some sense an
abstraction ; it is one step removed from the deciding
authorities. The I.M.C. is one further step removed from
those authorities and is in danger of being even more an
abstraction. With the central Secretariat split among
various offices, there is a tendency towards relying too much
upon the two strongest councils in the membership. Further,
the central standing committees of the I.M.C. meet fairly
infrequently, at least not frequently enough to take action
on immediate issues. All this means that the I.M.C. can
be in danger of acting too slowly, or only acting when it is
too late. It also means that a tremendous responsibility
rests upon the Secretariat ; this will and should always be
the case, but it can mean that too much depends upon the
particular bent and interest of a few persons.

Second, in line with what has just been said, it is characteristic of the I.M.C. that its history is indissolubly linked
with specific persons. It was people like Dr. Mott, Dr.
Oldham, Dr. Paton, Dr. Warnshuis and Miss Gibson who,
to such a large extent, formed the history of the I.M.C.,
and gave it its special ' face ', who won the confidence of
member councils and whose personal work in many respects
in fact constituted the work of the I.M.C. There is a very
real element of realism in this fact ; it was, in particular,
Dr. Oldham who constantly stressed the necessity of thinking
in terms of real persons, not just vague committees. It was
in line with this that Dr. Kraemer before Tambaram was
asked and given complete freedom to write his book on *The
Christian Message in a non-Christian World*,[1] and nobody can

[1] Edinburgh House Press, 1938.

doubt that this book has probably meant more than many committees. *But* everything then hinges upon the person concerned and neither Oldhams or Kraemers are too easily mass-produced !

Third, although this is a very dangerous generalization, it is perhaps permissible to say that, broadly speaking, the I.M.C. in its thinking and work, in its whole atmosphere, is characterized by a " western-mission-board-perspective ". This is not primarily meant as a criticism. The I.M.C. is not a new body ; it has a history behind it and cannot start with a *tabula rasa*. It inherits that history and cannot and should not run away from it ; but it should face it clearly. One element in the recent years' work of the I.M.C. (reflected also in the element of confusion at Willingen and Ghana, which also has a positive side) is undoubtedly a real struggle with this and attempts to get into a wider perspective.

Finally, a fourth characteristic can only be hinted at here. With the particular structure and *ethos* of the I.M.C. it is difficult to speak about any theological line which in a special way has coloured the I.M.C. Indeed, it can be said that a real presupposition of the existence of the I.M.C. was that theology was left out of the debate. This, of course, is only partly true, and it is certainly not true any longer. It was, however, made clear from the beginning that questions pertaining to the doctrinal and ecclesiastical differences between Churches were to be outside the orbit of I.M.C. work. This was no doubt the only way in which the whole thing could have been started, and it is not without interest to note the rôle which—indirectly—the Evangelical Alliance then played in the formation of the co-operative agency. Co-operation seems to a large extent to have been the key word in the I.M.C., and this is a large step compared with non-co-operation and rivalry. Yet it is a very real question whether the I.M.C. can escape a critical study of the underlying concepts. At the Willingen meeting in 1952 the I.M.C. was asked to pay particular attention to what was called " internationalization ", e.g., instances and experiments in international and inter-confessional missionary co-operation. This means more than the technical or organizational side of the matter. In handling this subject it will be necessary for the I.M.C. to discuss frankly a whole series of theological questions which traditionally have been labelled " Faith and Order ", but Faith and Order issues are to-day also " missionary issues ". Co-operation can be undertaken on the tacit assumption that there is no real conversation about the things that unite and divide ; in the long run this will not unite anybody. Where missionary work is more than technical and economic assistance to other churches but is directly engaged in Mission, there the issues of Faith and Order are an integral part of Mission and cannot be shirked.

There are many other characteristics of the I.M.C. which should be mentioned, but this must suffice here.

With this background we shall briefly look at some aspects of the situation to-day. We shall here limit ourselves almost exclusively to the material which was produced in connection with the Ghana conference.

2. SOME GHANA REFLECTIONS

The writer is strongly tempted here to say to himself : " I will leave this whole section blank ! Let the reader read all the Ghana material earlier in this volume and then read Prof. Freytag's brief speech again in the light of all this, and reflect on it. He will find questions raised which may do more than this whole essay." Nevertheless, we must try to reflect a little on some of the issues raised in the Ghana material. It is difficult if not impossible to get a clear picture ; the material is patchy and uneven, and yet it reflects remarkably clearly some of the fundamental questions with which the world mission to-day is faced.

There is no blueprint for action. The questions are there, but it cannot be said that Ghana gave real answers to them. In the deepest sense there exists no blueprint. There is no ready-made plan which we can catch hold of if only we are clever enough or radical enough. It was perhaps possible to write a more or less water-tight " Missionstheorie " forty years ago, but it is highly questionable whether this can be done to-day. We are all involved in a structure which is changing ; we stand in the midst of this, and our task is to try humbly and patiently to find our obedience in the given situation. This task is upon all of us, in the west and in the east, and we can only discharge it together, by listening together to the Word of God, by being part of one another in a new way, carrying one another's burdens, sins and forgiveness. We shall make mistakes and we are making them all the way. Can they also receive the forgiveness of God and the forgiveness of the brother ? Impatient radicalism can sound impressive in its one-sided clarity, and it may cut a Gordian knot here and there, but it will not solve our real problems which have to do with our basic obedience at this hour. It is said in one of the papers that, being human, we are more likely to go too slowly than too fast ; let us not forget that the opposite possibility also is there, that we may go too fast, escaping our real points of obedience. It is not the clever brain which will help us in the end ; more is needed than that.

Reading through the Ghana material again, one gets the impression that it is really all variations on a theme, variations from quite different situations and individuals showing different approaches and different problems, but all variations on the same theme : " the Mission of the Church "— or, to use a sharper phrase, " the One Mission of the One Church ".

This one theme was set within the context of papers and discussions on the scene within which this Church exists and to which it is sent. Particular attention was here paid to issues like the witness of the Church in and to the social-cultural structures in which we live, and to questions concerning the proclamation of the Gospel to men in the non-Christian religions. The major concerns, however, seemed to be on this main theme. This may seem to be introversion and self-interest. It was not meant to be so by the planners of the conference, nor was it really introversion which characterized the atmosphere of those discussions. There was uncertainty and confusion and even more, there was a deeply felt inner need and pain in many of the deliberations. We see the tremendous tasks ahead ; we see the challenges and the opportunities. The only thing we want is to try to meet those challenges, to proclaim the Gospel to those who are outside the Church. And yet, it seems as though we cannot do so. Why ? How can we together find the way forward, find a new liberation in obedience, find new joy and conviction ? Such sentiments were underlying much of the discussions and it is against this background that the over-arching theme must be seen.

A basic presupposition in all the discussions was what has been said a hundred times before individually and in official statements of ecumenical bodies, that " Mission belongs to the very *esse* of the Church " ; we have said this so often that perhaps we are simply taking it for granted now without struggling further with it. It is true, but what does it mean ? This sentence is taken by some as the theological reason for the proposed integration of the I.M.C. with the W.C.C. In the west it plays a prominent rôle in discussions concerning the relationship between missionary societies and boards and their respective Churches ; in a very large number of cases it has meant that the missionary society has become an organizational part of the Church concerned. All this is well and good, but is it all ? Much too often in the thinking of missionary societies it has meant that mission is not just the responsibility of the few, the specifically ' mission-minded ' people, but that it is the whole church which must support the missionary society. Again this does not go far enough. It means at least two things, closely intertwined.

First, and perhaps with specific regard to the west, it puts a serious question to the missionary society or board in its relationship to the Church of which it is a part. The real question here is not primarily an organizational one. One mission leader from the west puts it like this : " Our missionary society is no longer the only or main point through which our Church has its connections with the churches in Asia or Africa ". A whole picture is changing here. Not so very long ago—and in a number of places it is still the case—the mission board was virtually the ' foreign department ' of the Church through which connections with the churches in Asia and Africa were channelled. This is changing, and rightly so. Increasingly a series of activities of a humanitarian character find their outlet at other points and through other channels. Official church connections are less and less channelled through the mission board. It is to some of this that Prof. Freytag refers in his speech : " For a long time the societies have been unique in their work, in the sense that they were almost the only bridges for the service to foreign people. This was the reason why they gathered among their supporters many who felt a mere social responsibility to foreign people and not a specifically missionary one. Now that uniqueness is no more. They have their activity among many other activities, which are missionary in some sense, but in very different expressions. That means that many people who share the sense of the missionary responsibility of the Church do not find the way to share the work of the societies." The mission board will have to wrestle with its own nature and task ; how can it really help its own Church to become not only ' mission conscious ' but a missionary church ? This is not achieved by mere organizational integration of the mission into the church structure, nor is it simply a question of securing more interest and support from the whole church for the work of the society or board.

Second, saying that Mission belongs to the *esse* of the Church means more than securing the official stamp and control of the church upon missionary activity. It means something about the church's understanding of itself in its own situation. The church—the local church—is a part of the world mission as this is being unfolded in God's hands ; the witness, the existence of this local church in its particular local situation is a witness, an existence *in* the world mission. It does not live for itself. Its witness, its obedience in its own situation participates in God's world mission, is a part of the witness of the body of Christ, is heard and seen by the other and perhaps weaker members of that body ; and it is possible, in spite of all missionary activity, to betray that world mission—at home. If Mission is at the centre of the very essence of the church, then it is not just an added activity ; then it means accepting in deepest earnest a constant inner tension in the church itself, a tension which constantly forces the church beyond itself, which denies it any self-affirmation, confessionally, denominationally and otherwise. To accept that Mission belongs to the *esse* of the Church means the beginning of the renewal of the Church, and such renewal takes place under the Cross.

This is of absolutely fundamental importance for any discussion of plans and relationships in the world mission.

In the discussion at Ghana about the mission of the one Church there was a constant referring back to the Whitby phrase about " partnership in obedience " and considerable discussion about its contents and implications. It was stated again and again, and where it was not said it was the underlying assumption, that the missionary responsibility rests upon the whole Church, that every member of the Church has the obligation and the right to proclaim the Gospel to those outside the Church.

For one who has never been a missionary it is perhaps dangerous to touch upon the following, and yet one's thoughts go back to a number of visits to churches in Asia and Africa, and in particular to the meetings at Prapat and Ibadan, Nigeria. It is difficult to underrate the significance of those two meetings. There were many and quite different trends and aspects noticeable in those gatherings, but one thing was overwhelmingly clear, that the driving power, the compelling force, was a deep conviction that the Church—

however small and however weak—is there to carry the Gospel further afield. It was said clearly and repeatedly at Prapat that " there is arising in the Churches of Asia a strong sense of missionary responsibility, a compulsion to share with Christians in the evangelization of the world " (to use the words of the Bangkok Consultation in 1956). This has been repeated in a number of other statements from Asia during recent years. The same conviction was clear at Ibadan. It broke through whether the discussion was about the political and social structures or whether it was an African from East Africa telling about the Revival movement. A conversation with a Sudanese professor of history at Khartoum springs to mind : he said : " Remember that when you say history, you instinctively think back into what has passed into traditions and heritage ; for us history begins to-morrow ! " At Ibadan there was something of the same looking forward, not cheap optimism, but a firm confidence that " for us history is now beginning ".

Undoubtedly this increasing sense of missionary responsibility has something to do with the whole cultural and national development in those countries. Several of the papers in this volume illustrate this most clearly. Being a citizen of one's own country, accepting its destiny together with fellow-citizens and accepting responsibility for the shaping of its future also means accepting responsibility as a Christian citizen and throws one mercilessly into this responsibility. Picture after picture of such churches come to mind, small or large local churches where something of this was beginning to happen—and it was happening deep down below the level where official statements are made. It was happening through inner tension, uncertainty, mistakes and groping for light and direction. A new world was breaking into a village in the form of new political, social, economic forces ; a structure was breaking up and new values were beginning to count. At first sight it might appear to be simply destruction, a breaking down of what had been there ; yet, there was more than destruction in it.

There were the points of disturbance where decisions and stands are taken. The question was put again and again : " What does it really mean to be a Christian *here* ? " The question was put in all spheres of life, in the family, in the relation between parents and children, relation to community, etc., etc. There were the young Christian students who were not only studying in order to get positions with higher salaries, but in order to be of help to their country and their people ; they were just as strongly nationalist-minded as everybody else ; and here, precisely in this context and in the meeting with their Hindu, Buddhist or Muslim fellow-students the question again arose : " What does it mean to be a Christian *here* ? " There was a new responsibility behind the very question. It might be a question put in conversation to a foreigner and yet, in the deepest sense, it was not, and it would have been mistaken for the foreigner quickly to try to give the answer, because that question he could not answer and, had he answered, it would not have been an answer to the real question. No, the question was a question to the questioner himself ; he only tried to use you as a kind of mirror through which to gain greater clarity of his own picture, to find his own answer which was not to be in terms of an intellectual proposition, but in a concrete act of obedience with all its risks.

Here, somehow, is the " partner in obedience ". Taking all the risk of being misunderstood, it is necessary to underline this side. " Partnership in obedience ", the one mission of the one Church, all this does not first and foremost mean organizational arrangements ; inter-nationalization is not necessarily the same as partnership. This does not mean that new organizations are not necessary and that we must not try to experiment even drastically in this field ; but it does mean a humble warning that it is perfectly possible to construct new organizational buildings which are really just new embodiments of precisely the same thinking which produced the old. They may be adjustments only and not new and real obedience. Their very newness may for a time disguise the fact that they are old.

One essential requirement of partnership is that the partner must be a true partner, must be himself and as such give of the grace and forgiveness he has received. Is this partner from Asia and Africa *really* heard ? There is much glib talk about the situation being the same everywhere, in the west and the east, and therefore we must be equal, so equal that nothing must be said which does not apply everywhere, and therefore does not apply anywhere. In one sense all this is true, in another it is not. Partnership is not only a question of autonomy, important though that is. It is much more a question of selfhood. The situation in a church in England, Sweden or America is not the same as in a first or second generation village church in Central Africa, a church in a ' desa ' in Java, a church in India or the Near East. It is not that the one is better than the other, or stronger than the other (it may be larger but not necessarily stronger) or more mature than the other ; these are not the questions. There is sin and betrayal in the largest and in the smallest church, and there is obedience, but precisely where obedience becomes concrete (and therefore real obedience), there is the difference. The structures are different ; the heritages are different, not only the historical facts in our heritage but much more the heritage ' in our bones ', that in which we breathe, which is indissolubly involved in our deepest links and loyalties with our fathers, families, the very soil out of which we come. These differences do mean that we need one another. The witness of one part of the body is also the witness of the whole. The suffering, the failure and the rising again is part of the whole body. We have said for years that one church cannot answer the Word of God in the forms of thinking and expression of another ; this does not mean that these forms of thinking are therefore irrelevant, but it does mean that the response to God's call must come in one's own obedience.

This means that the churches in Asia and Africa must be taken much more seriously ; partnership means listening to the partner, to what God is saying through him to His Church.

What has been said here is pitifully inadequate ; there is so much, much more which should be said about a side of our partnership in obedience which is so fundamentally important and yet we must—regretfully—leave it here. Only two brief remarks more.

It is perhaps not completely out of place to call attention to the fact that there *can* be a danger in our ecumenical discussions and structures at this point. Striving towards producing " Christian opinion " and agreed statements we can encourage uniformity. There is as yet not nearly enough real Asian and African participation in our thinking and work in the ecumenical movement. The last few years have seen a rapid increase in this, but it must continue, and it is not done just by putting a few Asians or Africans on a committee where the thought categories, the whole tenor and rhythm of the conversation, is western ; the result may be that we are " bringing younger Church minds to bear on the dilemmas of the west rather than compelling the west to concern itself with the most vital problems of the younger Churches " (to quote an early document in the I.M.C.-W.C.C. discussions).

Another point in this connection. Prof. Freytag said in his paper that " the younger Churches cannot conceive of mission without imitating western missions, in a positive or a negative way ". While this is true, it is also true to say that in these Churches, perhaps not so much in organized form as in the ordinary life of the local church, missionary obedience is constantly groping for realization at new points and in new forms. We have talked much in recent years about " new forms of Mission ". This is important, but perhaps it is essential in this sphere also to listen carefully and patiently to the voice of the local churches in Asia and Africa, their voice in obedience and disobedience, and to try to discover where the points of obedience are and what that means for the ' new forms ' of Mission in which churches in the west and the east are going to be engaged.

Another aspect of this partnership in obedience, the one Mission of the one Church, can only be hinted at here. Several of the papers deal directly with this question. It comes up under the name of " Inter-Church Aid ", " New Forms of Mission ", Christian Councils, and perhaps most sharply in Graaf van Randwijck's paper, in which the questions are put with refreshing honesty and clarity. They are sharp and cannot be avoided. Ghana did not give answers to these questions and they *must* be studied further. Closely connected with this paper is the paper by John V. Taylor on " The Place and Function of the Missionary ". No attempt will be made here to go directly into these specific questions. There are, however, one or two things which may be of some relevance here, although to state them means running the risk of trying to say something which is difficult to formulate clearly in a short space.

In the beginning of his paper Graaf van Randwijck says that it only deals with " a minor problem in the whole context of this world-wide movement ". It may, however, point most sharply to one of the very real issues. It has again something to do with the fundamental nature of the partnership in obedience. The paper referred to raises the question of whether missions should perhaps be modelled upon an " inter-church-aid " pattern to produce greater efficiency and perhaps to remove some of the apparent difficulties in missionary relationships with the churches in Asia or Africa ; it also at least hints at some of the implications of this. It is quite possible in some areas and at certain times and with specific kinds of operations that the " inter-church-aid " *structure* may have to be applied to ' missionary ' operations, but is there not more in a missionary relationship than " spiritual technical assistance ? " A bank in Nairobi can ask a bank in England to send out a specialist to help it in a specific matter for a given time.

There is complete equality and the man concerned is in the service of the bank to which he has gone. If the terms of service or the conditions under which he has to work do not suit him, he can quit as he likes. The two banks concerned are entirely equal and independent, making a working arrangement for a given time to give the one the help it needs. But there is much more or rather something entirely different involved when we talk about " partners in obedience " and under obedience. At the risk of overstating the matter and of being misunderstood, it can perhaps be said that in the " inter-church-aid *perspective* " the partners concerned are basically left unquestioned. They can still be independent units. Their autonomy is preserved and it can even have the effect of self-affirmation. In the " missionary perspective " the partners are no longer unquestioned. Their autonomy is caught up in a different kind of " belonging together ". They are both deeply questioned in their deepest being and obedience. Where one church enters into ' partnership ' with another in a missionary obedience which points beyond both, there they are dependent upon one another in the despest sense, and autonomy is questioned by obedience. It must be stated most emphatically that the two ' perspectives ' referred to do *not* automatically cover the two phenomena known as " Inter-Church Aid " and the work of the mission boards ; we are not here basically talking about organizational structures but about underlying concepts and driving ideas. The point is precisely that much of what has been and is being done by mission boards may fall under the category of " inter-church-aid perspective " and the " missionary perspective " may to-day, in many instances, find a true expression in " Inter-Church Aid ".

But in thus talking about the autonomy of the church being questioned by this partnership in missionary obedience are we not contradicting what was said above about the self-hood of the Church ? Perhaps, and yet it is possible that the selfhood is endangered precisely by the ' aid ' which affirms the autonomy, and that the ' missionary ' partnership in

real obedience will help *both* churches to find their selfhood,
to become " the Universal Church in its local setting "
(to use an expression from Willingen).

All this may sound very nebulous. Perhaps it is ; yet
it seems certain that, together with and underlying all our
attempts together to find new expressions for missionary
obedience to-day, there must go real and frank study
and discussion of these other aspects. It is all part of
saying that " Mission belongs to the *esse* of the Church ".
In the light of such considerations, the very difficult
questions must be asked (not in general but in the particular
situation) : How does a church use the missionary serving
in its midst ? What is *his* ' selfhood ' ? How does the
church give this missionary the spiritual and pastoral care
which he needs more than ever ? How does the Church
(or its mission board) select and prepare its missionary to
be sent out ? What is the picture he is given of his task ?
How is he prepared to serve in obedience ? How can the
two Churches together loose themselves into new obedience,
plan together and obey together the call to proclaim the
Gospel to those who are outside the Church ?

3. The I.M.C. and the Ecumenical Movement

The purpose in this section is not to sketch the history
of the I.M.C. and its relationship to the development of
the other streams in the ecumenical movement, nor to
outline the developments in the relationships between the
I.M.C. and the World Council of Churches. This has been
done fully in a number of other places where this material
is easily available. Rather, a few comments are made on
this subject as it looks to one person.

It first needs to be said that the I.M.C. is a quite fundamental part of the whole ecumenical movement, and
therefore the above title is really misleading. This needs
to be said because one can find in a number of places a
tendency to separate the two. In stating this so emphatically, we are not only referring to the influence of Edinburgh,

1910, nor just to the significance of subsequent missionary
conferences, nor primarily to the influence of the I.M.C.
as an organization, although it had a most significant part
to play in the very formation of the W.C.C. We are
thinking more of that for which the I.M.C. stands, the
Mission of the Church to the world. This is no specific
prerogative of the I.M.C., and yet in the formative years of
the ecumenical movement the I.M.C. focused it particularly
sharply and gave an impetus and an impatience which were
needed and healthy. In the whole I.M.C. structure in
which, as we have said earlier, there also are weaknesses,
there was and is a demonstration not only of regionalism
(or whatever the modern phrase is) but of something much
more important, of the necessity for accepting the ecclesiasti-
cally unacceptable and illogical in the world mission of the
Church. The world mission of the Church is something
more than the combined activities of our recognized
Churches. This needed to be said and it still needs to be
said ; this inner tension is a part of the whole ecumenical
movement and must continue to be so.

With the formation of the World Council of Churches in
1948, the three major streams in the ecumenical movement
met, although the organizational relationships were of a
somewhat varied nature, the I.M.C. being only " in association with " the W.C.C. The formation of the W.C.C. did
not mean everything was streamlined, but it did mean that
precisely in the meeting of these three streams, new questions
were raised and new perspectives were realized.   " Faith and
Order " issues are being seen in other and new contexts,
and even in the case of the I.M.C., where the relationship
was looser, the same was the case ; we have seen it at every
turn of the road since 1948. The " in association with "
relationship has not only meant clearance and consultation,
but changes, new problems and difficulties, new perspectives
and vistas.   It is no mere accident that a document on
" The Mission and Unity of the Church " had to be written.
This was not just engineered by the relationship between

the two councils ; but much more fundamentally it arose from the very deepest nature of the ecumenical movement itself. Nor is it an accident that it is increasingly being said that the W.C.C. is not only concerned with the unity of the Church but in and through that with the ' renewal ' of the Church ; this is where mission and unity meet and this is where the W.C.C. and the I.M.C. belong together and cannot get rid of one another.

Although the question of the relationship of the I.M.C. and the W.C.C. does not constitute the major theme in this essay, it is nevertheless impossible to discuss the rôle of the I.M.C. at this hour without giving some consideration to this matter and expressing one's views on it, however imperfectly. We shall leave aside the whole organizational discussion, as this is explained and discussed in a number of other publications ; a full report of the discussions which took place at the Ghana meeting is available and will throw light on at least some of the questions involved as seen from the side of the I.M.C.

It is necessary here to stress again that these views are strictly personal and do not represent anybody but the present writer.

We shall not comment upon the arguments put forward in this discussion ; we have no right to do so here. Our only task can be to give a few comments upon lines which to us seem to be important ; these will be rather disjointed and sketchy, but there is not room for more than that.

First, and in general, it is necessary to say quite frankly that this is an exceedingly important and serious hour for the I.M.C. ; this may sound like a platitude but it is more than that. We have tried in the previous pages to point to some of the issues and problems involved in the world mission to-day. Those issues and problems are the I.M.C.'s, and in facing them the I.M.C. may have to leave known and well-trodden roads and venture into the unknown. It is possible to try to live out of the obedience of the fathers— and this may be the danger and temptation of the I.M.C.

at the present time. The discussion at the various I.M.C.
conferences from Edinburgh to Willingen, the statements
produced by the I.M.C. about the theological nature and
basis of Mission—the I.M.C. now stands at the point where
it will have to take the consequences of all this, and there
will be consequences, whether the answer to integration is
'Yes' or 'No'. Either set of consequences may be
costly. There are clearly risks involved. Let it not be
forgotten that there are also risks involved on the side of
the W.C.C. ; but we have here no right to speak on that
side of things.

The risks may be costly. Some member councils of the
I.M.C. may feel compelled to withdraw their membership.
This is profoundly to be regretted and the I.M.C. will be
the poorer for it. It is to be hoped that the present plan
will provide sufficient flexibility in its structure to allow
for various modes of relationships and thus to retain a
practical fellowship. There are a whole number of other
risks, but will we really reach our decision by weighing
risks and costs ? (Which does not mean that the most
careful attention should not be paid to them.) The I.M.C.
is not just an organization which can do as it pleases in its
own interests. It exists for a purpose which is infinitely
larger than itself, and therefore it is compelled by its very
nature to pay the fullest attention to the situations and needs
of its member bodies, while at the same time—in the fullest
consultation with and fellowship with all those members—
deciding on its course in obedience to its purpose and calling,
which again are larger than all its member bodies combined.

At least to one observer this means that the I.M.C. must
say 'Yes' to integration. (It must be remembered that
the I.M.C. is only one partner in this question ; there is as
yet no decision on the side of the W.C.C.) It is not suggested that integration will automatically solve all the
questions which the I.M.C. is facing. On the contrary, it
has earlier been suggested that integration in itself will not
really solve anything, but that it may provide the frame,

the setting for seeking solutions and answers. This means that it may be after integration that the I.M.C. is faced with its real challenge.

There are organizational intricacies to be worked out and this is not exactly easy, but one may hope the problems are surmountable. We make only one comment on this ; it is essential that some constitutional form can be found and agreed upon whereby the I.M.C. structure with its council relationship will be accepted into the combined organization as a living part of the whole. This is important not just in order to preserve something which has been considered valuable in the past, but because something of rather fundamental importance is involved. The Councils are of quite different nature and composition in the various areas ; in a few places they are definitely church councils, in most they are not ; among their members there are missionary societies which are virtually independent of their own Churches, inter-confessional missionary societies and various other voluntary Christian bodies. It is not suggested that such councils should be able to speak for the Churches, but it is suggested that a relationship be developed which can give them not only a certain structural affiliation, but real responsibility. It is fully realized that this particular point is extremely difficult and that it may prove to be the crucial point in the whole matter. This is one of the places where the risks arise (for both organizations) in taking fully seriously that the Church is a missionary Church. There is an inner illogicality here, an inner tension which is in tune with life itself. Can that be accepted ?

It has been said—one hopes as a result of tiredness—that the amalgamation of the I.M.C. and W.C.C. means the burial of the I.M.C., and that " this body is dead anyway, so let us accept integration ". It may be true, but surely this line of argument will not lead us anywhere. The reason for integration is certainly not a ' selling out ', but an attempt to find the way forward in honest obedience to what is right. There is an inner compulsion and necessity in the very development of the world mission as symbolized in the whole I.M.C. structure. It is difficult to see how—if integration does not take place—the W.C.C. can avoid developing its own ' missionary arm ', not as a reaction to the I.M.C. but out of obedience to its own nature and calling. If it is to be a full World Council of *Churches*, if it is to work wholeheartedly for the ' renewal ' of the Church, will it not have to have world mission at its very centre— or betray the statements of *both* the W.C.C. *and* the I.M.C. during many years of their history? Again, if this were to happen, the logical continuation of the I.M.C. would be such a new missionary development of the W.C.C. What would in that case remain as a separate I.M.C. organization would be a different entity from what it has been hitherto. It would be the continuing I.M.C.—continuing in separation—which would be the *new* body, not the Division of Missions in the W.C.C. This has to be faced clearly.

But more compelling to us is the very nature and situation of the I.M.C. and its whole task within the ecumenical movement. We have suggested that in a number of ways the I.M.C.'s most urgent question has to do with the very nature of Mission itself, and that that is not only a question of working out new ways of missionary operation and organization but raises a series of fundamental theological questions as well. Will not a setting within the W.C.C. provide us with a better framework for doing that than we have at present? Do we not need the whole context of Inter-Church Aid, Faith and Order, and all the other concerns of the ecumenical movement to come to our own clarification? Are we not under an obligation to carry Mission into the very place where the Churches meet as churches? Is it not in this very meeting that we have to struggle with the calling to Mission? It is possible that the I.M.C. may receive more from all this than it is able to give, not least in regard to the discovery of the nature of Mission to-day.

4. The Rôle of the I.M.C.

It is a reckless adventure to try to say anything about the rôle of the I.M.C. at this time. Here, if anywhere, the picture of the Scottish hills from the introduction applies : as soon as one thinks that the hills are in sight then the rain is certain to fall and to blot out the picture immediately ! Yet nobody engaged in the work of the I.M.C. can escape the responsibility for trying to look ahead in an attempt to see what are the main tasks of this body in the years immediately in front of us. It is more likely than not that we shall be proved wrong. Things are moving too fast to make it easy to produce long-term plans. But responsibility demands the attempt, for discussion and criticism.

The rôle of the I.M.C.—that in a sense is the same as it has always been. The aims of the I.M.C. are not radically changed, but it is possible that there are different emphases, new aspects and new expressions to be given to those aims in this present situation. Let it be said right away that the task of the I.M.C. is not less important in the years ahead than it has been previously. The I.M.C. is not going out of business. It has still a task to do and one which is perhaps considerably more difficult and complex than it was a couple of decades ago.

In the following discussion of the rôle of the I.M.C. it is assumed that integration is going to take place and that we are talking about an I.M.C. within the structure of the W.C.C. ; *so when, in the following paragraphs, the term 'I.M.C.' is used, it stands for the I.M.C. as continued within the W.C.C. structure.* This, of course, is a big assumption, but it seems to the present writer impossible to say anything at all about the I.M.C. in the years ahead without assuming this. If this integration does not take place, it seems utterly impossible to predict what organization we are talking about when we say 'I.M.C.', and therefore impossible to say anything about its functions and tasks.

(a) *Some General Remarks*

Before going on to a more detailed discussion we may be allowed a few general remarks which to some extent will be a repetition of what has been said at various points earlier in this essay.

First, a few reflections which may seem to have mere structural reference, but which nevertheless point considerably further.

We can think and discuss about integration in terms of the merger of two organizations where all the technical intricacies involved in differences in constitutions and organizational structures will have to be considered and worked out ; all this is necessary. Everything that the two organizations stand for will have to be preserved and continued in a new form. In the proposed plan of integration much has been done to ensure that the various elements which have characterized the life of the I.M.C. will be preserved under the new structure. This is undoubtedly right and necessary at the present stage.

And yet it is necessary to face clearly that there is infinitely more involved in the proposed new structure than just the preservation of the traditional lines of the I.M.C. We have said at various points that Mission in one form or another is at the heart of the ecumenical movement itself. We have hinted at changes which have taken place within the I.M.C. itself during the last twenty years or so. Activities which twenty years ago naturally belonged to the I.M.C. (perhaps because there was no other international body to deal with them) increasingly and in different forms have been taken over by other streams within the ecumenical movement. We have tried to indicate that the phrase " Mission belongs to the *esse* of the Church " has far-reaching consequences for the Church itself, for its whole conception of its own nature and calling. All this comes into the picture here again. Perhaps one may say that what is involved is *both* a widening of the missionary perspective or dimension *and* a concentration ; a realization of the fact that Mission is not

224 THE GHANA ASSEMBLY

just a special type of activity which can be identified and circumscribed within a mission board or a special Division of Mission, but is something which has to do with the very existence of the Church, with its very *raison d'être*, with its not being for itself but for the world, to the ends of the world and the end of time, that every element of the Church's life and existence is a part of this ' sentness ' to proclaim the Cross and the Resurrection to and in the world, whether it has to do with the Christian witness in the sphere of politics, of social-economic questions, of health and education or anything else.   Here it is not just a matter of " the attitude of the Church " or of " what has the Church to say ? "   (Along these lines the Church can so dangerously easily become another power factor, the real power of which lies not in its message but in the numerical and influential power behind the message ; perhaps there are elements in this which ought to make us constantly submit our activities, our statements and their intentions and motives in these spheres to careful scrutiny.)   Here also the Christian existence has its central purpose and meaning in the proclamation of *the Gospel* and that is not the same as the " Christian attitude " or the " attitude of the Church ". All this means that Mission is involved here.   It is the perspective within which all this points beyond the Church, itself, and makes it impossible for the Church to speak from its own safety to the world in a kind of self-protection.   In every aspect of this existence there must be the missionary dimension and call.   And yet at the same time as the perspective is widened there is need for concentration.   We have not said that everything the Church does is Mission, but we have said that in the very existence of the Church, and therefore in everything the Church says and is and does, there must be a " missionary perspective ".   The need for concentration is precisely here, in the working out of this problem, in the constant calling to Mission in and through the various aspects of the Church's life, the calling to *missionary obedience* in the Church's dealing with political and social problems, in the Church's evangelistic activity, in its constant theological struggle with questions of Faith and Order.

Let us put this in another way with more specific reference to the proposed integration.

The Divisions and Departments of the W.C.C. should not primarily be thought of as units within themselves, as mathematical figures ; they are rather parts of a body, an organism rather than an organization. This way of putting it may be a slight idealization ; perhaps too often one meets the organization rather than the organism ! This is nevertheless the picture we must have in mind and try to realize ; the other tendencies will have to be fought. In this case we are introducing through a Division something which—we say—belongs to the very centre of the whole body. We are not introducing something new, something which has not been there before ; we are rather realizing and taking seriously that Mission is a fundamental concept in the life of the W.C.C. This also means that this new Division will not have any monopoly of ' Mission ' ; there will constantly be activities, in all the other Departments and Divisions, discussions, studies, underlying concerns, etc., which can only be termed continuations of what twenty years ago were accepted I.M.C. concerns. This should not disturb us ; on the contrary. This is precisely what is desired and to be aimed at. Fear has been expressed lest ' Missions ' should be ' departmentalized ' and shut up in one little corner of the whole building. This, naturally, must not happen, but perhaps it is not the real danger ; perhaps the real crux is whether the proposed Division, which will bear the specific name of Mission, will be able to give to all the other rooms in the building what they will need and want to have ; the ' shutting up ' can come from the Division itself rather than from its neighbours.

That there exists a Faith and Order Department does not mean that therefore Faith and Order issues do not come up in the other sections of the W.C.C. nor that they cannot be considered by these other sections. We should not here think in ' departments ' but in ' points of concentration '. The task of a new Division of Mission and Evangelism is not to take charge of everything within the W.C.C. which comes under those headings—precisely not—but to be the ' point of concentration ', where specific attention is given all the time to these matters, where they are studied and discussed, where advice and consultation takes place, from where new impulses and initiatives can come.

One more aspect of this. With the amalgamation of the I.M.C. with a *World* Council of Churches an interesting and important change of perspective *can* take place. For a mission board in the west, Mission (whatever its theological interpretation) in practice means lines going to Asia, Africa, Latin America, etc. The I.M.C.'s member bodies in the west are Missionary Councils in one form or another, and the I.M.C.'s concerns in the west have been and are with the work of the mission boards or churches in their work in those areas abroad ; this, of course, is oversimplified, but it still describes the picture sufficiently clearly. Naturally all this is not going to be changed over-night. Integration does not mean starting afresh as if there were no history. There are organisms which will have to grow together slowly and patiently ; therefore, the outward picture may not change so very much for a considerable time to come. And yet, there can be a change of perspective. Within the World Council there may be a manifestation of what we have said so often, that Mission is not just from west to east. The Division of Mission will not necessarily be the point where knowledge of Asia and Africa is concentrated ; there will be other sections and committees where we may find more representatives from the Churches in those areas than in the Division of Mission. Here we shall be confronted with the question : what is the I.M.C. doing about Mission in the west ? What is really Mission ?

There is another line which must be mentioned again here. We have seen earlier how the I.M.C. grew up as a body of councils representing and reflecting quite different situations, and we have pointed to the necessity of including this conglomeration of different structures in the new combined structure of the two bodies. There are at least two things to be stressed here.

First, we have said that the importance of this stems from something more than just preservation of a traditional structure, nor is it simply a matter of accepting the council-structure as such ; that is no more sacrosanct than any other structure. Perhaps one may quote here from an early document in the W.C.C.–I.M.C. discussions about 1948 :

> All the member-units of the I.M.C. (N.C.C.s, national missionary conferences and councils) include within their membership (i.) churches which will for long remain outside the W.C.C., either on grounds of conviction or because they have not yet reached the degree of autonomy required for membership ; (ii.) missionary societies, inter-denominational in their basis or but slenderly related to any organized churches. It must be emphasized that the part played in the total life of the I.M.C. as well as in its national councils, by the two categories just described, is quite vital and must not be impaired . . . the significance of these national organizations which compose the I.M.C. lies in the fact that for the primary purpose of the Council (the furtherance of the world mission of the Church) these local federations are imperative. All the most urgent tasks and concerns of the I.M.C. call for this close local inter-working of every agency concerned in the missionary enterprise. Confessional differences, even the distinction between Church and Mission, are subordinate to this.

What is hinted at here is that this whole structure is necessary, not just from a strategic point of view but that *for the sake of mission*, in the missionary perspective " even the distinction between Church and Mission is subordinate ". This is perhaps not exactly a happy phrasing of the matter ; what is meant (one presumes) is that in its missionary obedience the Church is caught up in God's unfolding of His history of salvation, becomes a part of that drama, points at every stage beyond itself (and in thus losing itself becomes in a new way the Church of Christ in this place). In this pointing beyond itself the Church must take seriously the working of the Holy Spirit also in places and in forms which do not easily ' fit in '. Here we as churches are concerned with more than ourselves. Here we are under an over-arching obedience to proclaim the Gospel to the world. In that perspective we must consider very seriously the issues involved in the amalgamation of the untidy I.M.C. structure with the W.C.C. structure ; they both need one another and it is to be hoped that a very real amalgamation can take place.

Second, the I.M.C. structure involves de-centralization, a real emphasis upon the local situations. Although it should not be overstressed, there is real significance in this. We have already earlier emphasized the importance of the " selfhood " of the local situation, and need not say much about it here. Again, this is not just for strategic purposes but because there is something here which has to do with the essence of the proclamation of the Gospel—the proclamation of the Gospel to people and peoples, the Church's own obedience and witness in its own political, social, cultural and religious structures.

It is in this kind of context that we must discuss the rôle of the I.M.C. within a new W.C.C.–I.M.C. structure.

Practically speaking it is obvious that the I.M.C. will have to continue many of the activities which at present are carried out under the auspices of that body. Perhaps one may venture to suggest that—in the case of integration —a very critical look be taken at all the things which at present appear on a full I.M.C. agenda, in order to see whether or not some of them here and there could not profitably be handed over to other agencies and perhaps be done better by them.

At the same time, however, the central rôle of the I.M.C. in the coming years must be—to use a vague term—to " call to Mission ", not just to carry on traditional activities

but to wrestle in a fresh and bold way with the meaning of
Mission at this time, to struggle with the question of the
structural embodiment of that Mission in the given situation,
to find new ways of obedience, to experiment and, where
necessary and possible, to take upon itself responsibility for
such experiments. This " calling to Mission " also means
becoming deeply involved with the other aspects of the
W.C.C. structure. Precisely as a " point of concentration ",
the I.M.C. must be closely related to Faith and Order.
What does the missionary perspective mean for Faith and
Order discussions ? What has Mission to say about the
issue of unity ? Why exactly is it that the strongest impulses
towards unity come from the so-called younger Churches—
and what is the real significance of this ? We need a real
conversation on these matters, for the sake of both partners.
The same applies to the other sections in the ecumenical
movement. We should not expect that the " calling to
Mission " is the special monopoly of the I.M.C. nor that it
will come exclusively or perhaps even most strongly from
that section, but surely it is the special responsibility of the
I.M.C. to go wholeheartedly into precisely that and to
accept that responsibility with all it involves.

(b) *Some Illustrations Concerning the Rôle of the I.M.C.*

One of the major contributions of the I.M.C. has been
the building up and strengthening of Christian Councils in
various parts of the world and constant help in co-ordinating
and strengthening co-operation in the world mission. A
most impressive number of organizations and institutions
owe their origin to the direct or indirect influence of the
I.M.C. This type of work is an integral part of the I.M.C.'s
activity and must continue ; yet it is possible that the rôle
of the I.M.C. here is changing in character and perhaps in
size. There is still a very real work to be done in this field ;
there are areas where the Christian Councils are weak and
need strengthening, and there are territories like Africa and
Latin America where some kind of regional secretariat is

being discussed. At the same time one can ask : what does it mean that an East Asia Christian Conference is being formed ? What does it mean that an increasing number of National Christian Councils seek affiliation with the W.C.C. and in increasing measure are related to and channels for the various ecumenical activities going out from the W.C.C. ? Is it possible to suggest that the rôle of the I.M.C. as such in this structural sphere will be diminishing in the years to come ? Even in the cases mentioned above, where councils need strengthening or where new formations may come into being, these matters are no longer the sole or perhaps even main responsibility of the I.M.C., and in several cases can only be handled in the closest co-operation between the I.M.C. and the W.C.C.

The I.M.C. is by its constitution " advisory and consultative ". If we add ' only ', then the terms take on a negative tone : the I.M.C. has no mandatory power or right over its members, it can ' only ' advise. But those terms need not be fences around the field of the I.M.C. ; they can be positive liberations. It is possible that the central rôle of the I.M.C. is precisely within the area of " advice and consultation ", taking those terms in their deepest sense and with real responsibility. Although one here probably ventures beyond the limits of the permissible, it may nevertheless be relevant to say that, if this is taken seriously, then it is so much more necessary that the central and responsible committee of the I.M.C. meets more frequently than the present constitution provides for ; its task is not just to pass resolutions or to authorize new developments or the actions of the Secretaries, but to be a body of informed and representative people which, at the centre of the I.M.C., is in constant discussion and consultation about the purpose of the I.M.C. and the basic issues with which it is dealing. With the decentralized structure of the I.M.C. this body at the centre is necessary. What is suggested is that the major rôle of the I.M.C. in the years to come lies mainly within the area of advice, study and experimentation. There may be nothing new in this, but then the criterion is not whether it is new or old.

With this as general background let us venture to say a few words about the rôle and tasks of the I.M.C. as they appear to one person. This will, naturally, not be an attempt to make a sketch of a whole conglomerate of I.M.C. activities ; nor is it the suggestion that the following lines should necessarily supersede what is being done at present. In other words, it is *not* the idea that what is suggested in the following constitutes the whole of the rôle of the I.M.C. —very far from it. But it is suggested that perhaps it is along some such lines as the following that the most important task of the I.M.C. will be found in the years immediately ahead.

It has been suggested above that perhaps the central rôle of the I.M.C. should be found within " advice ", and not primarily in the sphere of structure and co-operative organization. This is said with all due caution, well knowing that there is still a considerable responsibility in this sphere. Nevertheless, we are now talking about the particular Division of World Mission and Evangelism within the W.C.C., trying to see where its *main* rôle is to be played within the world Mission.

The theme of the Ghana meeting indicates the fundamental rôle of the I.M.C., and at the centre of that stands the studying of and grappling with the very basic meaning of Mission. We have used the term " the calling to Mission " —in all its aspects and in our situation to-day. This means a variety of different lines and activities which can only be hinted at here. It means study, education, experimenting in action, consultation, etc.

We have already indicated how this calling to Mission forces the I.M.C. into a fundamental conversation with the other " points of concentration " within the W.C.C., with Faith and Order, with Church and Society, with Inter-Church Aid, with the C.C.I.A., etc. There is a very real task here which must be taken very seriously. In every case it concerns the Church's understanding of its missionary task and the way that is to be discharged in the particular sphere.

There are all the various ways in which the I.M.C. tries to help in the world mission, giving advice, help and information where possible. In and through all that, the I.M.C. ought to give clearer voice to " the unfinished task " ; a term which has receded somewhat into the background during recent years, perhaps through too much concern, or a wrong concern, with our own problems. This is not just a matter of giving population figures, but much more of setting all our discussions within that context of the missionary obligation.

At the centre of it all, however, still stands the necessity for coming to grips with the meaning and structure of Mission at this hour. Perhaps one may put it sharply and say that the I.M.C. will fail at its most central point if it does not regard this matter as one of the most fundamental, if not *the* most fundamental, task at the moment and over the next few years. We cannot " call to Mission " with conviction and a good conscience unless we are clearer at this point ; it is a dilemma, but must we not accept the dilemma and the pain it carries with it and try humbly and with courage to find the way forward in obedience ?

This will mean study, plenty of study, but lest we be misunderstood, let us say immediately that the intention is not to turn the I.M.C. into a " study department " as that term is technically understood. We do not refer to purely academic study but study as an integral part of every operation, a constant watching and analysing of where a particular operation is leading us, what it teaches us, where it goes wrong.

Over recent years the I.M.C. has already given considerable attention to this question and has at least tried to find some way of entering into the heart of the matter. It has not proved to be exactly easy. On the contrary, it is exceedingly complex and we should be careful not to oversimplify the matter in order to make it manageable as a study. It involves study and discussion, the most careful study of Biblical and theological realities, and equally careful study of the complex situations and the practical and hard factual issues with which the Churches and Missions are struggling in their " partnership in obedience " ; it involves study and discussion of organizations and structures. If, as we are here contending, the most important calling of the I.M.C. at this hour is to give real help, leadership and advice in this field, then this must be given the most prominent place in an I.M.C. agenda for some years to come and we must be prepared to expend money and personnel on it.

Although this is not the place to discuss the detailed issues involved, one may perhaps suggest at least three lines, or rather major areas, within which this question may have to be pursued simultaneously.

There is first a Biblical-theological study line. We need very real study here and the widest ecumenical discussion. We need Biblical scholars and theologians who will help us in this matter and who, together with mission and church leaders from the east and the west, will grapple with those questions. We need to do all this in the closest conversation with the other aspects of the ecumenical movement. We need the W.C.C. studies in " The Lordship of Christ over the Church and the World " and the studies in " The Authority for Evangelism " ; we need the other divisions in this conversation.

There is another line of a different character. It is study, but something much more than study. It concerns the structures of mission as these appear in the practical, concrete situations, both in the west and the east (the missions board and its church, the concepts underlying the board's work as part of the church, the way in which the mission board also says " Mission " to its own Church, the practical relations of mission to church, new developments in structure, and a host of other questions). This matter

needs real study, but not just academic study ; the process
itself must engage those responsible for policy and decision,
and the process itself must endeavour to find and test
those " new forms of mission " which missionary obedience
in concrete situations is being led to accept.

The third area is intimately related to what has already
been mentioned. The term " ecumenical mission " has been
used very much during recent years, sometimes exceedingly
superficially. There are very difficult theological questions
involved in the concept, and yet there is a reality here which
needs careful consideration, both theologically and structurally. There are significant developments in the picture
which must be followed closely. We are thinking of, for
example, the new East Asia Christian Conference, the experiments within the Lutheran World Federation in various
types of co-operation, or, more recently, the All Africa
Church Conference in Nigeria and its proposed Continuation
Committee. There are several other types of experimentation going on at present. These are more than attempts at
' regionalism ', in reaction to a certain type of centraliza-
tion. There is within them a realization of a missionary
obligation, of the necessity for coming together for its sake.
It is possible that within them there may be a new context
for the mission-church relationships, where a bi-lateral
relationship can become a multi-lateral responsibility. This
is fraught with difficulties and pitfalls, but it may be that
the I.M.C.'s most important structural responsibility lies in
this field, in trying to see whether or not the calling to
Mission at this hour also involves such totally new structures
as can only be achieved within such multi-lateral formations.

There are obviously many other lines which should be
mentioned here but these will suffice to indicate the contours
of the rôle of the I.M.C. in this field. We have suggested
above that the central committee within the I.M.C. should
play a much more significant part in the work of the I.M.C.
May we suggest here that these various lines be made the
special concern of this committee, that they in a very real

sense meet here? They are different in form and character, and in the daily work of the I.M.C. will run along different lines, but their focal point is the question concerning the meaning of " the Christian Mission at this hour ". They should constantly be watched and studied and discussed as they throw light on the central question. In the central committee (whether this is the Administrative Committee or the Commission) the issues involved in them must be the object of constant discussion and deliberation.

In his paper Prof. Freytag tries to draw some consequences from his previous deliberations and says, " In all the facts there is a clear lead towards concentration. I am not going to discuss priorities. I think of concentration in the deeper sense in which by way of the changing situation God, so to speak, concentrates us. . . . Does God not make us free for the more difficult but essential task, to concentrate on the message of Christ Himself, which means on the message of the Cross? " This is what this central concern of the I.M.C. is about.

We further suggest two other matters of a slightly different kind. First, to a large extent under the influence of the I.M.C. a series of ' study centres ' have been set up in the Near East, India, Pakistan, Ceylon, Hong Kong and Burma, and others are under discussion. Their task is—roughly speaking—to study the meeting of Christianity with Hinduism, Islam, etc., in the specific situation and to help the Churches in their witness to man within these religious structures. We venture to suggest that these centres represent another aspect of the rôle of the I.M.C. ; their potential importance is very great indeed and their work should be a special concern to the I.M.C. More is involved from the I.M.C. than just helping in the setting up of these centres ; most of them are now beginning to find their own feet and to secure at least some essential staff. The time is then coming when they must be given all the help possible in the very formulation and conception of their task. At the same time there is a study being formulated (by the present Evangelism Department and the present Missionary Studies' Department) on " The Word of God and the Living Faiths of Men " ; both this study and the centres for the study of non-Christian religions must be seen together and be part of one another.

Second, although it is difficult to put into a clear programme, the I.M.C. has a considerable rôle to play in the finding and training of ' leaders '. This cannot be done by setting up a committee, but is a personal matter of finding the right men and making sure that they get the right background and training. Here the closest co-operation with the Ecumenical Institute at Bossey is necessary. Another aspect of this is of paramount importance. The I.M.C. has—as indicated in the Ghana reports—received a very considerable sum of money for theological education in the lands of the younger churches, and two special committees have been set up to function under the I.M.C. in this sphere. There is no doubt at all but that what is beginning to take form here can become one of the most influential aspects of the rôle of the I.M.C. Hand in hand with financial help in the building up of theological education, there ought to go the most careful study and discussion of the very meaning of theological education in these situations, its form and character, its aims and purposes. We have earlier, in the discussion of partnership, emphasized the need for real mutuality, for meeting the true partner and for real selfhood. This also has relevance here ; it cannot just be a question of transferring western theological curricula or of translating western theological textbooks. While this cannot and should not altogether be avoided (no church starts *de novo*, nor can it neglect the history of the Church universal), it is of fundamental importance that the best theological help be given the Churches to wrestle with their own questions as they see them, feel them and are tempted by them—and to find their own answers !

And finally may we mention *as a question* another category. The I.M.C. has always refused to become ' operative ', to undertake missionary work directly itself. On several occasions there has been pressure to do so, but it has been withstood. This is undoubtedly a perfectly right principle : this responsibility rests with the Churches and missions and must continue to do so. And yet, is it not possible that at this hour there are areas and concerns where the I.M.C. as such ought to be ready to assume also ' operative ' responsibility, temporarily and experimentally ? With the Orphaned Missions Fund during the war the I.M.C. did a most significent piece of work which might not have been done had the I.M.C. not been there ; it did not become ' operational ' in the technical sense of the word but came closer to it than ever before. With the new Theological Education Fund the I.M.C. has again assumed such responsibility, and that in an area more sensitive and more close to the essence of the Church's ' selfhood ' than most others.

Is it not possible that there are in our situation experiments and first attempts in new advances for which the I.M.C. should be ready to take direct responsibility ? Such responsibility should—and this is essential—only be delegated responsibility. It should be of an experimental character and should never become permanent in its nature. Churches or missions might in a given situation ask the I.M.C. to undertake on their behalf an experimental task involving action with the clear agreement that, after a given time, the Churches and missions will take over the task completely in one form or another. We shall obviously have to be extremely cautious in this field and yet it should not perhaps be dismissed altogether.

As an illustration may we mention the question of an approach to Islam in Africa. It is possible that the I.M.C. could be asked over, say, a five-year period to study and explore the situation and to get people with special training and background to go into specially appointed tasks within the Churches in the areas concerned in Africa. There might be teams working on specific aspects. It would involve courses, meetings and discussions with African pastors and church leaders. Every step would have to be taken in the closest consultation and co-operation with African Churches, Christian Councils and missions, but the over-all direction of such a plan might be in the hands of the I.M.C. for the preliminary time mentioned. This is only an illustration which may be appropriate or not ; there are undoubtedly other aspects which might be closer to the suggestion or more easily applicable. This is simply put forward as a question to which the answer may be " No ", but it is hoped that it will receive serious consideration before that answer is given.

There are many other things that should and could be mentioned ; as said previously, what has been suggested must not be taken primarily as a programme but only as illustrations of the kind of concerns and activities which would characterize the rôle of the I.M.C. It must again be underlined that these suggestions are made with regard to an I.M.C. integrated into the W.C.C., and therefore pay particular attention to those *specific* tasks which a Division of World Mission would seem to have within this larger whole. There are many other aspects of the present I.M.C.'s work, which in an integrated structure perhaps would not to the same extent be the specific concerns of the I.M.C. Again, nothing has been said about the other element within the proposed Division of World Mission and *Evangelism* ; this has not been our task here, but that does not mean that it has not been taken into account in suggesting the above matters for specific consideration.

(c) *The I.M.C.'s ' Location ' within the W.C.C.*

According to the present plan it is proposed that there be a Commission (corresponding to the present I.M.C. Assembly) and a " Division of World Mission and Evangelism " which will work under the mandate of the Commission alongside the other Divisions within the W.C.C. This ' location ' is of some interest. There has never been any doubt about the status (division or department) but there has been discussion about the relationship between the present Division of Inter-Church Aid and Service to Refugees, the present Department of Evangelism and a new Division of World Mission. The present proposal is that the two latter be combined into one Division while the first remains as a separate Division. This is a good arrangement. The nature of the work of the Inter-Church Aid Division demands a special kind of organizational apparatus and it might be too complicated to have the two combined. There is, however, at the same time a special relationship between these two divisions. There is a conversation between " Mission " and " Inter-Church Aid " which must not only go on but go deeper ; the ' wall ' between the two divisions must at least be so low that one can by sheer ' mistake ' now and then find oneself in the other ' camp '. The presently proposed combination of Evangelism and World Mission may not be so easy as it seems on paper and yet they should be together. The present Evangelism Department, under the Study Division of the W.C.C., and the I.M.C. are very different bodies in structure and sentiment, but they must belong together ; they need one another and there is also here a conversation which must begin to take place but which has hardly been started yet.

Although it is not the place here to talk about the implications of integration for the location of I.M.C. headquarters, it should nevertheless be said that this matter must not be taken lightly ; it is of tremendous importance for the whole task and psychology of the I.M.C. In the view of the present writer the headquarters should be in Geneva with only contact-points in London and New York. At the same time there should be much more direct contact with Asia, Africa, Latin America. Utmost mobility is essential to the carrying out of this work and no amount of correspondence can be a substitute. This mobility is demanded by the basic lines we have suggested at various stages in this essay, the necessity for working *in* the situation, for being in the closest possible contact with developments, modes of thinking and

experiments.   It might even be suggested that I.M.C.
Secretaries should be prepared to spend considerable time
in one or another of the regional areas, making the regional
Secretariat their headquarters for several months.

The rôle of the I.M.C. is, as it was when it was formed,
to call the Churches to their missionary task, to help where
possible to a clearer proclamation of Christ.   The task is
not to build up the I.M.C. organization, but to make it
serve Him in obedience in the situation in which we stand,
trying to hear His call to us through these situations and
through our own uncertainties—and then to follow the call.